MANGO AND MINT

Arabian, Indian, and North African
Inspired Vegan Cuisine
Nicky Garratt

Photography by
Lena Tsakmaki

Mango and Mint: Arabian, Indian, and North African Inspired Vegan Cuisine
by Nicky Garratt
© 2013 Nicky Garratt

ISBN: 978-1-60486-323-9
LCCN: 2012913631

PM Press
PO Box 23912
Oakland, CA 94623
www.pmpress.org

Cover design by Nicky Garratt layout by John Yates/www.stealworks.com
Layout by Jonathan Rowland
Photography copyright © 2012 Lena Tsakmaki except front cover and page 239

10 9 8 7 6 5 4 3 2 1

Printed on recycled paper by the Employee Owners of Thomson-Shore in Dexter, Michigan.
www.thomsonshore.com

Contents

First Bite

I came to vegetarianism quite unaided, as far as I remember. Prior to 1970, the year that my memory flags as the beginnings of my cruelty-free awakening, my diet was already quite nonconforming. I detested eggs and fish and recall being at Filbert Street in the mid-1960s watching Leicester City football team play while eating hot dogs sans sausage. Oddly, from a quite early age I also shunned chocolate along with most other candy. When Easter rolled around, both of my brothers awoke to a large chocolate egg waiting by their beds, while my treat was an extra-large bag of peanuts. It wasn't until I was in my forties that chocolate worked its charms on me. My family were, and remain, quite mainstream in their thinking when it comes to food, and I was certainly the outsider. The origin of my views was philosophical, challenging injustice, hypocrisy, and irrationality. Our family always had pets, and when I was a child Pinky the guinea pig happily occupied the guard coach of the toy train as it was pulled around the garden. Our Alsatian dog was trained to help us off with our socks at bedtime, and years later Sophie the Pyrenees mountain dog was like a member of the family. Yet it seems that I alone saw the dichotomy between the elevated life of these pets and the lamb or pig on the plate.

Starting in the mid-1960s, I'd become increasingly interested in the cavy (guinea pig) world. I started tentatively breeding the Himalayan variety and expanded to other breeds. My father and I modified a wooden outbuilding, which we placed in the back garden. He fabricated multiple metal hutch doors for the rows of cages built like deep shelves along one side. These roomy deluxe cavy apartments were modular and a simple slide out divider doubled the size of each unit. Along with a sow pen, the system accommodated around 40 guinea pigs. By the '70s I was not only going to shows, transported by my dad, but eventually became a judge. Maintenance was time-consuming. Most days I was out pulling grass and weekends the cages were cleaned. During the summer a giant wire enclosure, with divisions for boars, was moved daily across our lawn for grazing. I have to conclude that the experience shaped and was shaped by my feelings about animals to some degree. Certainly I had no intention of ever betraying my obligations to these creatures.

As I entered my teen years, the last remnants of meat faded from my diet. I can't say there was a specific date attached to it, but certainly by the time I was playing in real bands I was a full-fledged vegetarian. I suppose the counterculture that eventually awaited me in 1977 was a good fit for a nonconformist but at the time, too young for the prior hippy movement, I was on my own.

I stumbled into my first band in the early '70s, meeting the bass player through the guinea pig shows. It was a short-lived, longhaired, three-piece, proto-prog/heavy rock band. I think we were called Holliday. Actually the name was quite irrelevant as we fizzled out without a debut show. I do remember converting the drummer's parents' living room into a rehearsal space while they were away on vacation. We dragged the furniture out, then pulled off mattresses from the beds and lined the walls. The bass player, somewhat older than I, mumbled through some arbitrary lyrics, bookends for endless riffs and solos. The band is almost forgotten, even by me, save that I learned two things. First, that block rehearsal trumps the once-a-week get-together, and second, when you strap on a guitar girls want to kiss you.

Through that period I was also jamming with a couple of schoolmates. In due time we found a drummer and turned into a blues band called Piltdown Man. We did one or two gigs, which we put together ourselves and rehearsed that standard blues repertoire which had launched so many '60s British bands. The singer, Simon "Honeyboy" Hickling (who later went on to play harmonica with the DTs, Steve Marriott, and Bo Diddley) was devoted to the blues. I,

on the other hand, was more interested in the emerging hard rock/progressive scene, particularly in that transition period once those bands had left 12-bar structure behind and the compositions became more expansive.

"Roll" Model

By 1974 I moved on, playing in a six-piece pick-up band a short drive across the border in Northamptonshire. The band was put together initially for a village barn dance but struggled on for a while thereafter. The dance itself was memorable in that we had to haul the upright piano, affixed with roller casters, across the fields on the back of a flat cart pulled by a tractor. What could go wrong? Anyway, the project inherited a benefactor of sorts in the form of a man who had designed unique equipment for the disbanded local rock band Stonewall. David, then age undetermined, was mostly retired from a high-profile position with Marconi Radar. (When we recently caught up via e-mail, he was 96 and still an herbivore.) Using his already-existing innovative sound system, I was recruited to wire a channel for the new mixing board.

This interesting character's life was filled with extraordinary events, people, and objects—the great British eccentric if you will. He had an enormous influence on me and would venture to great lengths to find exotic food items and prepare them in an exacting manner. I recall that, I think by virtue of contact with one of the developers, he possessed a microwave oven, in the mid-'70s. He owned a large old brick house on the corner of a quiet lane surrounded by a high brick wall. Various food items were often cooling on a kitchen table while a dozen hand-built beehives provided jars of honey stacked in an outbuilding. In another outbuilding sat a half-finished sports car, which he was assisting a local to build from a kit, yet another housed a gas-powered laser in the loft space above. This contraption, the size of a washing machine, could fire a beam through a trapdoor in the roof into the foggy English night sky. Besides introducing me to avocados and Jerusalem artichokes, he also exposed me to the music of Wagner through his monolithic electrostatic speakers standing in the living room.

Back in Leicester I was playing in a heavy rock outfit called Hole. After about one uncompromising year of rehearsals, the bassist and I began earning money as the backing musicians for an older singer playing the social club circuit in a variety act called Albatross. This circuit was a mixture of mostly working men's clubs, with a few Liberal, Conservative, and British Lions clubs thrown in. We played two or three times a week at our peak, mostly on weekends. Between gigs we created a new "serious" progressive band. Of course the "real" band had no gigs but with the addition of J.B. on sax (later of Dexy's Midnight Runners—who was not a party to our mercenary project), we eventually made the big move down to London together just in time for the punk explosion. Within only a few months I joined the embryonic UK Subs.

The early punk scene in London was one of those magical times in the history of art when we all felt something special was taking place, and I dove headlong into it. Every day there was something new in the scene and, although we didn't give it much thought at the time, those events eventually became legendary. The gigs with the Subs escalated from local pubs, the Marquee, the 100 Club, the Roxy, and the Vortex, to large national tours, then to major international excursions within a couple of years. TV and press kept pace with our charting records. By the late '70s we were opening for the Police in the United States, followed by a European Ramones tour in 1980. From then on it was headlining only. It was an amazing whirlwind ride. One unforeseen consequence, however, was my vegetarianism colliding with the practicalities of touring. This logistical challenge ultimately motivated the documentation of these recipes.

Where's the Leaf?

Traveling around the world over the past 35 years, I witnessed significant improvements in the accommodations for vegetarians and even vegans. There's no doubt things improved but my early years as a professional guitarist were often burdened by constantly trying to track down food.

In the larger upscale hotels or restaurants it seemed the kitchen staff had no notion of a vegetarian cuisine and those who chose a meat-free diet were obliged to yield to a plate of steamed vegetables, maybe some sort of soy cutlet, or the dreaded tofu. At the other extreme the "in-house" chefs for venues across Europe and the United States, while usually understanding the meat-free concept, often served up what could best be described as hippy food. When the promoter declared that the cook made a great vegan curry, it was a good day for the diet. The "curry" was normally a huge pot of stewed vegetables with a couple of cans of coconut milk and a few tablespoons of curry powder thrown in.

Other culinary mainstays of the counterculture were the catering-sized bowl of overcooked pasta laced with mixed vegetable cubes, or the salads of shredded lettuce, cabbage, and carrots swimming in dressing. Many times I've been faced with undercooked peppers stuffed with rice and watery ratatouille while across the road sits a falafel take-away or Indian restaurant. This wanton state of affairs was only exasperated when traveling with not-so-like-minded colleagues. Then the reasonably accommodating dining opportunities, perhaps Mexican or Italian, were inevitably rejected in favor of a steakhouse or sushi restaurant. Still, I was ultimately quite content after the convention of stopping at a supermarket was gradually introduced and, armed with a "tuck bag" and various plastic containers, parking lots and hotel rooms became my diners.

Biting Back

In this book I try, in some small way, to take on this culinary drift by looking to traditional dishes that have always been vegan. The two ingredients in the title represent flexibility and creativeness of two broad branches of food preparation. Mango, in Indian cooking, is employed in both sweet and savory dishes as well as in drinks, while mint, similarly, in North Africa and the rest of the Arab world takes various roles as an herb in main dishes, for sweet tea, and in salads and sauces. There are thousands of sensational vegan options in these regions, which have been developed over hundreds of years, refined and perfected, and fit into larger palettes of complementary dishes constituting real cuisines. It seems to me that there is no need to make do, particularly in one's own home, by faking meat dishes or omitting the flesh to eat what's left.

Vegetarians and vegans will find the cuisines of India, North Africa, and the Middle East to be goldmines not only in flavor but also in color, texture, and aroma. In addition the flexible nature of their food presentation allows for great variety of utility. Unlike a meat-based diet, in which the kill becomes the center of a meal, a cruelty-free setting needs no such center. One can, of course, prepare a main course with side dishes but a spread with equal weight divided buffet-style works perfectly well.

This book is a manual for basic and more adventurous recipes from these regions with complementary recipes and additions. It is aimed at the parent whose twelve-year-old child has gone vegetarian or the omnivore host who has to manage vegan dinner guests. It is also an everyday book for the vegetarian and vegan whose diet perhaps needs a boost of ideas. While many of these recipes are based on authentic, traditional dishes, some concession has been made for the modern kitchen and occasionally some ingredients substituted to conform to a vegan diet, but only where it does not change the nature of the dish. The scope within each cuisine is by no means exhaustive; only select recipes are included. I have, however, taken care to include sufficient examples of each food genre to build a complete Indian, Arabian, or Moroccan menu.

I am not a professional chef or even an expert on these cultures, rather these recipes and ideas are the result of decades of fending for myself. While the religious nuances are surely wasted on me, I hope my reconnaissance—particularly in Pakistan, India, Lebanon, Syria, and Morocco—may occasionally enhance the tone of these recipes.

Dis-health-claimer

The reader might come to notice that I have not endorsed organic or locally grown food. The former is politically loaded and the latter a tall order for Far and Middle Eastern cuisine. I'll leave those notions to others, including the reader, to plug into these recipes or not as the case may be.

This is not a health food book, nor do I make any health claims about a vegan diet. Any health benefits from these recipes are purely coincidental. You will not read the phrase "supports the immune system," nor will I balance imaginary energy fields, attach fabricated properties to herbs and spices, invoke ludicrous homeopathic assertions, or any other such mumbo jumbo. I'm not qualified to assess vitamin or supplement needs but remain, for the most part, skeptical of the necessity to augment the diet in that way, although I'm told B12 should be supplemented in a vegan diet. Naturally there are some people who do have real allergies or other medical issues. To evaluate the merits of any diet I advise you to turn to an expert in the field, not a pseudoscience guru or for that matter a guitar player! My attitude in this regard is the blunderbuss philosophy: eat a broad variety of food.

My intention is to create a how-to manual, not a political manifesto. I believe I can make a strong philosophical case for a vegetarian or vegan lifestyle, but that is not my mandate here.

SUPPLIES

Some essential ingredients in this book are not always available in a supermarket. Most of the nonfresh components have a decent shelf life, though the spice mixtures should be stored in airtight jars, preferably out of direct sunlight, to retain a strong flavor. It should also be noted that certain ingredients can have different names depending on the cuisine. For example, fresh coriander is more often called cilantro in the West. Accordingly, I have tried to adopt the names most commonly used in the United States.

Besan

Indian chickpea flour (also known as gram flour) is a vital meal in India, where more than half of the world's chickpeas are consumed. It's used in batter, bread, desserts, pancakes, as a thickener, and even in drinks. It is made from the darker, smaller variety of chickpea called desi (which is also split to make chana dal) and comes raw or roasted. As dry roasting is quite easy, I recommend the raw flour, which gives more control and options. Besides the many recipes in this book that call for besan, it can have the additional use as an egg substitute in some recipes mixed one to one with water.

Black/Brown Mustard Seeds

In southern India these seeds are used to infuse cooking oil in a multitude of dishes, either at the start or at the tempering stage at the end—sometimes both! It is therefore important to have an adequate supply. I do not recommend substituting yellow mustard seeds for black. The higher-yielding black (or brown) seeds have a distinctive nutty taste once popped.

Coconut Oil

I've found that a mixture of coconut oil and canola oil is a good start for many

North Indian dishes instead of dairy ghee. Coconut oil's healthy reputation now appears to be restored, and health food stores usually stock this solid white oil. It is highly heat-stable and suitable for frying but can sometimes foam like butter, which reduces the heat transference. Often I suggest cracking mustard seeds in canola oil first, then adding the coconut oil.

Fava Beans (Dry Peeled)

Plunging them into boiling water for a couple of minutes helps to easily peel large fresh fava beans, but the large dried variety (fūl rūmī), are a little more difficult as they need to be soaked first. You can save a lot of effort by buying the peeled variety of bean. Peeling is not essential when using the small fava beans (hammām) but for falafel (page 101) and fūl mudammas (page 104) pre-peeled is painless and way better.

Oil

When a recipe in this book calls for "oil" (rather than olive or coconut oil specifically) use canola, soybean oil, or another light vegetable oil.

Peppers

Pepper heat is measured in Scoville Heat Units (SHU), capsaicin quantity. The modern rating method accurately measures the potency of peppers but is then converted to Scoville Units for common use. Wilbur Scoville originally devised his scale in the early 1900s using tasters to flag the detection point of the capsaicin extract from various peppers in dilution.

Peppers fall into a huge spectrum of strength from bell peppers, which register zero SHUs to staggeringly hot cultivated varieties way over 1,000,000 SHUs. For these recipes, I suggest serranos as a slightly milder fresh pepper, (5,000–23,000 SHUs) up to cayenne (30,000–90,000 SHUs) to give the dish some kick. A good idea for cayenne powder is to stock the best strength for your taste. I usually dry and grind my own cayenne. If I do buy powder, I use the stronger African bird's-eye variety listed at 90,000 SHUs, which I'm told can push into the 100,000s. If you want to moderate the heat of the recipes a little you can buy the milder American powder. That way you will not need to adjust the measurements and you'll save a little money.

Tamarind Concentrate

Tamarind fruit is a beige pod-shaped legume which is normally soaked in hot water to release the dark brown paste inside. It is then strained to remove the skin, fibers, and seeds. For large cooking projects calling for a lot of tamarind, this method produces the best and most flavorful results. However, it is messy and time-consuming and for 95 percent of dishes there are better options. Raw tamarind is also available in a block already stripped of the unwanted matter. This avoids the most arduous step in preparation, but be careful because some hard seeds are sometimes still buried in the block. For this book I have converted tamarind measurements to concentrate. Tamarind concentrate usually comes in a plastic tub and is a black, treacle-like substance. It keeps a long time in the refrigerator and is a very convenient form for use in home recipes.

Spice Mixtures

These spice mixtures can certainly be homemade, and have variations from region to region, or country to country.

However, seeking out every spice for the smallest amount will leave you with bags of unused ingredients, and if you have a store that carries these readymade mixes it really saves time and money.

Chaat masala: This mixture contains sulfury black rock salt, mango powder, and ground cumin along with other spices. It is used to flavor a number of Indian foods and is often sprinkled on fruit salad.

Garam masala: A spice mixture normally added to a dish at the end of cooking to add a warm, sweet finish and also to thicken the sauce.

Panch phoron: Five whole spices in equal amounts: cumin, fenugreek, mustard seeds, fennel, and nigella. This mix is popular in eastern India to infuse the cooking oil.

Sambar powder: This is a southern Indian curry powder mix. It is distinctive in that rather than the more familiar northern masalas, ground coriander seeds are used in far greater amount.

Za'atar: A mixture of powdered thyme, sumac powder, and sesame seeds. Za'atar is a mainstay of Lebanese cooking mixed with olive oil as a dip or bread dressing.

Fresh Ingredients

Fresh Curry Leaves

You can't really beat planting a curry leaf tree to provide a reliable supply of leaves, but many climate zones negate that option. My tree is in a container at a friend's house in a warmer zone. The leaves resemble bay leaves but are softer and smaller, growing alternatively along two sides of a sprig. Sometimes the dried leaves can be substituted, but fresh is best. If you don't have a decent Indian store near you, often an Asian supermarket will carry fresh curry leaves, but be careful—they are sometimes labeled as bay leaves. Also note that some garden centers carry a plant called a curry plant. It is silver grey and smells a little like Indian spices but is not a culinary plant. When you do find fresh curry leaves, they can be frozen for later use.

Fresh Methi

Methi, or fenugreek greens, are very pungent and can exude from the skin days after eating Indian food. It is not widely available in the United States, but I do find it at times at the farmers' market. When I find methi, I usually buy a lot, wash, trim, and cook it, then freeze it for later use. Substituting the ground fenugreek seed works in instances where the recipe calls for a tablespoon of dried green methi, but the main use of the fresh herb is to cook it like spinach. There really is no substitute but you can grow your own.

Equipment List

Spice Grinder

I strongly recommend a good spice grinder. Spices are stronger and more aromatic when freshly ground. It is much better to stock whole spices and grind when needed. A mortar and pestle is useful for small amounts of some spices, but for larger batches it can be a lot of work.

Iron Skillet

Indian food, with the addition of the tandoori oven, is typically cooked on the open flame using an iron skillet. I use a couple of everyday-size skillets and a giant one for batches or party cooking. There are lots of variations on how to season a skillet to make it nonstick. Some come preseasoned, or you can clean it with water, dry it thoroughly, coat it with vegetable oil, and heat it on the cook top. After your skillet has been seasoned, cleaning with soap is to be avoided. Instead clean with a scrubber and water, rinse, and dry on a burner.

Food Processor/Blender

A food processor and blender are interchangeable for some of the work required for this book, but many blenders are not strong enough to cope with some of the stiff pastes, and some food processors don't liquefy the way a blender does.

Juicer

A juicer fills a very different function than a blender or processor in that it actually removes matter rather than assimilating it. I use one to extract juice but also use the extracted pulp to make vegetable stock (page 17).

Kitchen Scales/Measuring Jug

It's fine for a seasoned chief to estimate with spices and herbs. Sometimes it makes sense because many recipes use a placeholder amount, particularly when it comes to cayenne pepper or other spices. What the author can't know is how spicy you like food, what variety of pepper you're using, or how old the cumin in your spice rack is. There are many variables, and with experience you can almost intuitively adjust to accommodate these factors. That being said,

you need a base measure to start with, and some weights and measures are crucial. So buy kitchen scales, a measuring jug, and a set of measuring spoons and you'll be set.

Griddle or Nonstick Pancake Pan

The biggest hurdle when making pancakes or griddlecakes is the quality of the pan or griddle. A less than effective surface will destroy any chance or creating a well-made Dosa (page 112). I would add that a flatbread pan is also a required piece of equipment. My kitchen designer gave me a frying pan fifteen years ago. She swore by it and she was right. It has raised circular ridges almost like the reverse of a long-playing record. It works very well for Roti (page 33).

Tagine and Majmar

Although not essential, the tagine retains the full flavor of the food and makes even the simplest of vegetable dishes compelling. The majmar is a small clay pot that holds glowing charcoal, whereas the tagine is a Moroccan two-piece clay pot that holds the food. It is possible to use the tagine in the oven or on a diffused flame on the cook top without the use of the majmar, however what could be better than to sit in the garden and cook your food right there on the table?

The tagine comes in a few different regional shapes but all have some variation on the high conical, or occasionally domed lid. You can buy them glazed or nonglazed, but make sure you have a real usable pot, not a purely decorative one. Before first use, it is important to season the pot. Soak the tagine in water for about 3 hours, then place it in the cold oven. For the unglazed pot only, coat the surface with olive oil and rub it in. Use half an onion to scrub the inside of the tray and cone. Now turn the heat to 350ºF and bake it for about 3 hours. The tagine is now seasoned and ready for use. Skipping this step will usually cause the tagine to crack during cooking.

To clean the tagine, scrub with water and perhaps a little vinegar. Do not use soap as it will impart an unwanted taste.

Techniques

Dry Roasting

Dry roasting is a technique used in Indian cooking. The process releases the flavor of various seeds and spices. Take a small dry frying pan or iron skillet and heat it over a flame. When it is hot, but not smoking hot, add your seeds or spice. Shake while it is roasting to avoid burning one side. Slowly roast the spices until they start to darken and release their aroma. Do not overcook or it will burn, and be sure to have another cold container ready to transfer the contents. It is not enough to simply remove the pan from the heat because it will remain hot and will further roast and perhaps burn the spice. Let the spice cool in a container ready for grinding or for use in a recipe.

You can also roast desiccated coconut or besan (chickpea flour) in this way. Do not overfill the pan. You should have only a ¼-inch layer at most. If you need to you can work in batches, but make sure you agitate the pan or skillet while folding the contents with a wooden spoon. The process is quite quick, perhaps a couple of minutes. The besan will take on a darker shade and the raw smell will abate while the coconut turns a cinnamon color.

Tempering and Infusing with Oil

There are generally two different stages at which infused oil can be used in Indian cooking, and sometimes both stages are used in the same recipe. The first is at the very start where hot oil is infused by cumin seeds in the North, or black mustard seeds in the South. Of course other whole spices can also be used or included in an infusion mix. It is usually a good idea to have the bulk of ingredients prepared and next to the cook top to add to the pan as soon as the seeds are cooked to prevent them burning. It is very important that mustard seeds are popped before moving forward. It is only then that the nutty flavor is released. The second point where oil is infused is called tempering. Here, oil in a separate small frying pan is heated and whole spices cracked, releasing their flavor. The oil is then poured over the dish. Some of the common tempering spices are black mustard seeds, garlic, cumin, curry leaves, and dried chiles.

Tagine and Majmar Cooking

This ancient cooking method brings out flavor like no other. Throughout this book, the recipes are offered using standard cooking techniques, but some dishes are flagged as tagine-friendly. You can easily invent your own tagine dish with whatever vegetables you have.

As mentioned on the previous page, the tagine can be used in an indoor oven, but an alternative method is the majmar, which should only be used outside. If you are using a majmar, load it with wood charcoal. I usually start with a little paper and kindling to get it going, but do not place the tagine over the heat until you have an even glow after the flames are gone. In Morocco bellows are typically used to speed to this stage, but you can waft the charcoal with cardboard too.

The pot should have enough liquid so the bottom does not burn. Usually a little olive oil is poured into the tray to start it. Try any combinations of onions, carrots, parsnips, garlic, chunks of cabbage, leeks, or other vegetables. Perhaps add bay leaves, rosemary, thyme, crushed caraway, or cumin seeds. Add a little cayenne pepper or paprika and some olive oil. Remember some vegetables like onions will release juice, but with others you might want to add a dash of vegetable stock to get you started. Then slow cook until the food is finished, perhaps 40 minutes. Sometimes ingredients can be added in layers on top during the process—perhaps almond slivers, golden raisins, or pine nuts. You can now place the tagine on a heat-safe mat in the center of the table, but remember that the cooking process is performed outside only.

Proofing Yeast and Kneading Dough

To make most leavened bread the first stage is to proof the yeast. This entails mixing together lukewarm water, sugar, and dry yeast powder. After about 5 minutes, assuming the yeast is still good, it will foam. It is then added, usually with more water, to the flour. Once the mixture can be gathered into a ball by hand, it is turned on to a floured surface for kneading. This stage is crucial to build gluten strands.

A usual kneading stage is 10 to 20 minutes. Keeping the surface and your hands dusted with flour, flatten out the bread by rolling it forward with the heels of your hands. Fold it over against itself and repeat using some force. Working in this fashion the dough will become springy and elastic. The next stage is to let the dough rise in a warm spot for an hour or so.

Salting Water

When boiling vegetables or pasta in salt water, most of the salt is poured away after cooking. The size and shape of the pot and its content all contribute to the volume of water and thus the amount of salt added. Therefore an idea of the concentration is more helpful, not the total measure. I almost always estimate the salt I add when boiling vegetables, bearing in mind that one can usually add salt later but one can't subtract it.

Peeling Tomatoes

For most recipes in this book the ingredients are not over-processed, but sometime I call for tomatoes to be peeled. The best way I know is to dunk each tomato into boiling water for a few seconds. Once the skin has cracked, you can fish it out with a slotted spoon. Let it cool a little and the skin will slip right off.

Hoarder

When it comes to food, I'm rarely out of anything that can be stored. I suppose I'm a hoarer in that regard. Perhaps it's because resources for the omnivore are by definition more available that I tend to acquire my provisions in bulk where I find them. Perhaps it was decades on the road as the sole vegan or vegetarian. Then it was wise to forage through the ample food rider at the show with the knowledge that the next day was an eight-hour drive through Serbia and Croatia.

In 1983, General Wojciech Jaruzelski's regime attempted to soften its hardline image by opening Poland to subversive Western music. Clearly the UK Subs were the men for the job, making us the first bona fide Western punk band to play behind the iron curtain. We spent a couple of weeks hopping from basketball stadium to basketball stadium in a coach led by our freewheeling promoter and the government agent/interpreter "Bob." The meat-free concept was never harder to explain than then. Former lavish restaurants often maintained their swanky menus but the reality was listed in a photocopied sheet in the back. Meat was essential to display value, and without it you were generally left with a potato. Fortunately for our tour manager Lozy and me, Poland had Pewex shops where dollars, yen, pounds, or Deutschmarks could procure goods not available in zlotys. There, we managed to get cookies or other nonpotato edibles and traveled like premature bag ladies surrounded by plastic containers and shopping bags.

Finding vegetarian supplies is really not a concern in present-day San Francisco, but we are creatures of habit, so I've tried to co-opt that predisposition to be more efficient and more frugal.

Ganging Up

Many recipes require soak time, shelling, or boiling. Perhaps ingredients are simply not available and the thought of seeking out dried apricots in the evening or firing up the barbecue before you can even start on the dish simply steers one toward a grilled sandwich. But really a sandwich is just assembling parts prepared in advance, and you can adopt this idea to maintain a more compelling diet. In fact, with improved planning, you can make the choice to jump in and cook much less intimidating.

Strategic forethought will undoubtedly reap benefits in time management and flexibility and save a lot of money, particularly when buying produce in season at a farmers' market or buying in bulk. Most fresh ingredients such as tomatoes, greens, citrus, and eggplants are best processed immediately before storing. For example, greens can be quickly boiled, drained, then frozen. A good tip is to freeze provisions like methi or spinach in premeasured amounts and labeled accordingly. About a cup is the optimum size for this type of ingredient. Using this method avoids having to hack through frozen blocks to comply with a recipe on short notice. Tomatoes are perfect candidates for planning ahead. In season, full-flavored, vine-ripe tomatoes are a steal at the farmers' market. I buy 20 pounds or so, peel, chop, stew, and freeze them for later use. There is no comparison between a pasta sauce made from this vibrant fruit and the lackluster supermarket alternative. Orange juice can be also harvested when citrus is inexpensive and then frozen. Eggplants should be snapped up when the price drops, fire roasted, bled, and the pulp frozen.

A similar tactic can be employed in the garden. Often, particularly in California and Florida, people have more lemons than they know what to do with and will happily let you pick some. A neat trick is to freeze lemon juice in an ice cube tray, then the next day remove and stack the cubes into a plastic container. If you can judge the size of the tray to equal the juice from one lemon per cube, then you will always have a source of lemon juice. For hummus, simply defrost two cubes. While you're at it, make a jar of Preserved Lemons (page 165) for later use. When labeling frozen provisions, remember to indicate along with the contents, the amount, and date processed.

Some dishes require the same starting ingredients so it's useful to save time by "ganging up" on prep work. Of course you can prepare or even buy chopped onion or garlic for a head start, but you can go much further than that. Indian food can be thought of as modular in a way. For example the warming spice blend garam masala has a lot of ground, roasted ingredients, making it impractical to prepare each time you need it. Instead you would make or buy a batch to be readily available when needed. As with all spices, particularly when ground, it's best to store them in airtight containers away from direct light.

The idea of pre-prepared elements is apparent in the North Indian–style takeaway, where an order of alou matter or mixed vegetable curry can be rapidly completed. To achieve this efficiency, a base sauce is prepared ahead of time in great quantities. This idea is also very useful in the home. Keeping a base sauce or two in the freezer enables one to quickly throw together an impressive meal when combined with rice and chutney.

THE BARBECUE

Some vegetables used in these recipes are first baked over an open flame. I built a brick oven for this purpose, but a commercial barbecue would work as long as you use charcoal and not gas. When you fire up the barbecue, think ahead to which other dishes you might want to make another time and plan accordingly, because once the fire is going you want to maximize it.

Squash

I usually roast a couple of acorn or butternut squash when I'm using my outside charcoal oven. They are the first thing to go in and the last to come out. You don't need to wrap them in foil or any such thing, but remember they are very dense. To cook them through without charring deep into the flesh, you want to keep them out of the direct flame as much as you can. In my oven I built rounded ledges in the corners for just that purpose, otherwise a couple of layers of foil under each squash will protect it. As the fire dies down you can remove that. When you can easily poke a fork deep into the squash, it should be ready. (In particular, try not to overcook spaghetti squash.) Let them cool before scraping out the pulp into a plastic container. Store it in the freezer.

Uses: Butternut Squash Soup (page 46), Base Sauce (page 24, replacing the rutabaga), and Spaghetti Squash with Peanuts (page 83).

Onions and Garlic

Like squash, large onions and garlic bulbs will need to go into the oven early, again avoiding the direct flame. Leave the skin on because it will give some protection to the usable layers.

Uses: Fire-roasted onions can replace fried onions on burgers or in falafel sandwiches. They are more flavorful and less oily. You can also chop them and use them for a garnish on Chana Masala (page 98) or simply add them to a salad.

Eggplants

Buy large, dense, unblemished eggplants. Don't use the Japanese or Thai varieties for this roasting procedure. They—like the small, white, egg-shaped ones—are often fried directly. Eggplants, like tomatoes, are fruit and do not have, as some people believe, a gender. The idea of the "male" eggplant, with the smaller navel having less seeds and being sweeter is more likely due to its timely harvesting. Nevertheless, the bleeding process will make either sweet enough, just make sure it is not bruised or discolored. Eggplants go on the fire once the flames have died down a little in the middle of proceedings. This prevents the flesh turning to ash, but fully blackens the skin at a rate that allows the inside to cook and then collapse. Start by pricking the eggplant around with a fork. Place them over the flame so the fire barely kisses the skin. You will need to rotate the fruit so it is evenly blackened. Use blunt, perhaps wooden, utensils to avoid breaking them up. Make sure the stem end is well targeted. Once each one is fully collapsed remove them carefully and stand them upright in a colander inside a bowl. They will be leaking juice. If you need to, pour away the juice as it collects in the bottom of the bowl to avoid the eggplants sitting in the liquid.

Wait for the eggplants to cool while bleeding away the liquid. You can leave them like that for an hour or so. Now separate the blackened skin, scraping all of the flesh into a container. Discard the stem and all the small flecks of blacked skin, but include any darkened flesh, which will provide the smoked flavor.

In the container the pulp will continue to expel liquid. Keep pouring that away, as that juice is culprit for the rubbery effect sometimes present in supermarket baba ghanoush. Without it, your eggplant dish will be sweeter.

Once a reasonable amount of juice has been drained, store the pulp in sealed plastic containers in the freezer. Again, store in measured amounts marked on the lids. For example 1½ cups for one portion of baba ghanoush or 2½ cups for baingan bharta. Once you've tried charcoal-roasted baba ghanoush you will not be able to go back to the bland supermarket variety.

Uses: Ajvar (page 137) Baba Ghanoush (page 58) and Baingan Bharta (page 94).

Chestnuts

Seek out the Italian chestnuts, not the Korean variety, which are much less expensive but have little taste. Roast the chestnuts on the fire's middle to late stages, when it is still hot with a nice glow. Pierce both sides of each with a sharp knife and lay out the nuts on the grill—though first make sure they don't fall through. Keep rotating them to evenly blacken the shells. They should not be completely black, more charred in patches. Roast too quickly and the insides will be raw, too long at high heat and the inside will be burnt, too slowly and the inside will dry out. Practice makes perfect.

Uses: There's not many a better snack than hot chestnuts. I also like to drop them whole into spaghetti sauce.

Corn on the Cob

Select corn that has no discolored or rotten kernels and husk. Place the corn directly above the fire, without wrapping in foil, but quite late so the kernels get lightly charred, not burnt. Using your hand, coat the corn with the grilling sauce (page 138). It takes only a couple of minutes to roll corn on the grill and cook it so it is still crisp but the sauce has cooked. Serve hot. Refrigerate the leftover ears for a couple of days or freeze them for later use.

Uses: Black Vegetable Medley (page 223).

Bananas/Plantains

Bananas or Plantains can be roasted in the skin and turned so they are evenly blackened. If you want to add some grilling sauce or flavoring, simply cut them in half lengthwise when they are almost ready and add the seasoning. Close them up and return to the heat to finish.

Peppers

All colors of bell peppers are candidates for the barbecue. There is probably no vegetable whose flavor is more enhanced by fire roasting. Place the peppers over the flame toward the end of the charcoal burn when an even flame is achieved. Too aggressive a flame will turn the whole wall of the pepper to ash. Turn the peppers over the flame until they are completely blackened and no patches of color remain. Let them cool a little and then put them in a plastic bag for a quarter of an hour. The skins should easily slip away. You can also run them under cold water and ease away the skins. Leave them in a bowl and let the liquid drain. Pat the peppers dry, remove the stalk end and seeds, and then cut into strips.

Uses: Roasted Red Pepper Bulgur Salad (page 144), Ajvar (page 137), Muhammara (page 73), Red Pepper and Tomato Pilaf (page 130), and Pepper Sauce (page 143).

COOKING IN BATCHES

Another way to gang up is soaking or cooking various legumes and grains in bulk. Chickpeas are already quite inexpensive and when you cook a huge pot of them in one go and use them for various dishes—such as Hummus (page 70), Persimmons and Chickpeas with Anise (page 117), or Chana Masala with Chiles (page 98)—it becomes very economical. They can be frozen with the cooking water as well. You can also make a double or triple batch of moong dal and simply temper with flavored oil as needed.

Fresh Herb Cheat

It's not always possible to get every fresh herb—like cilantro (coriander), basil, or mint—when you need them. If you tend a kitchen herb patch it alleviates this problem, but it is easy to get caught between the annual herbs like basil or parsley. A trick to cover any lapse is to chop and pack herbs into an ice cube tray and freeze them. You can mark each slot with a felt pen. Then if you need to add some fresh cilantro to finish a dal for instance, just pop a "cube" out of the tray. Make sure it is fully defrosted before serving the dal, of course. This does not really work for fresh garnish though.

Vegetable Stock

An excellent way to make a vegetable stock is to use the solids from your juicer. Make sure all of the vegetables are washed before proceeding. Any combination of carrots, beets, celery, and garlic solids are boiled in a large saucepan of water for about half an hour. Strain the liquid through a fine sieve into a plastic bowl, cool, and then store in a plastic container in the refrigerator if you are using it in the next couple of days or in the freezer for later use. This stock is a perfect starter for soups like Lentil Soup (page 49) or Butternut Squash Soup (page 46).

DEEP FRYING

Deep frying can be messy. Oil can spit out or drip, and your hands can be covered with flour or batter. Therefore when you are set up to make Pakoras (page 232) or koftas it's a good idea to maximize the process and minimize the clean-up. Certain deep-fried food items freeze very well, so by setting aside a couple of hours you can stock the freezer with Samosas (page 39) and a variety of koftas. Pakoras don't freeze well, so perhaps if they are on your menu for the evening, you could utilize the hot oil and make a batch of Split Pea Koftas (page 85) as well for storage.

Sometimes the frying process imparts flavor to the oil, rendering it unsuitable to be shared for some dishes.

Here is a list of suitable savory recipes that do freeze well and are candidates for ganging up: bananas (for Bananas in Nut Sauce, page 93), Red Cabbage Koftas, (page 119), Falafel (page 101), Lotus Root Koftas (page 110), Fried Onion Garnish (page 153), Samosas, (page 39), Split Pea Koftas (page 85), and Savory Indian Snack (page 80).

These are sweet deep-fried recipes that can share the oil: Donuts in Syrup (page 178) and Deep-Fried Batter (Jalebi) in Kewra Syrup (page 177).

Almond Syrup

Type: Indian
Preparation: Overnight soaking
Speed: Fast
Notes: This syrup can be used as a refreshing drink to accompany an Indian meal.

- ¼ pound raw almonds
- Seeds from 10 green cardamom pods
- 3 cups water
- 1 cup sugar

Soak the almonds overnight, then rinse them in clean water and remove the skins (they should easily pinch off with your fingers). Crush the cardamom seeds in a mortar, then process them with the almonds and a cup of water in a food processor until you have a smooth milk. Strain the milk through cheesecloth into a bowl, squeeze out as much liquid as you can, and return the pulp to the processor. Process the pulp again with another cup of water, then strain into the same bowl. Repeat the last step once more.

Pour the almond milk into a saucepan and bring to a boil. Add the sugar and simmer for 15 minutes to reduce the liquid a little. The syrup can now be stored in the refrigerator.

Uses: Kumquat Coffee Dessert (page 180), Almond Drink (page 209), Mango Lassi (page 211), and Carrot Desert (page 173).

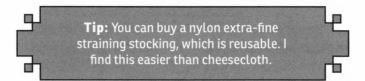

Tip: You can buy a nylon extra-fine straining stocking, which is reusable. I find this easier than cheesecloth.

Masalas

If you choose to grind your own masala powders, here are three useful blends.

Garam Masala

Type: Indian
Speed: Fast
Notes: Garam masala is a warming, thickening spice blend that is usually added to Indian dishes toward the end of cooking. Here is a basic mix, but there are many slightly different variations.

- 2 tablespoons cardamom pods
- 5 tablespoons coriander seeds
- 5 tablespoons cumin seeds
- 2 tablespoons black peppercorns
- 2 tablespoons whole cloves
- 1 whole nutmeg, grated
- 2 3-inch cinnamon sticks, broken into pieces
- 5 bay leaves

Remove the cardamom seeds from their pods and discard the pods. Dry roast the ingredients over low heat while shaking them for about 10 minutes. The spices will start to release their aroma. Do not burn. Grind the mixture in a spice grinder to a fine powder. Store the garam masala in an airtight container away from the light.

Chaat Masala

Type: Indian
Speed: Fast
Notes: Use to sprinkle on Indian fruit salad.

- 1½ teaspoons cumin seeds
- 2 black peppercorns
- ⅛ teaspoon carom seeds
- ¼ teaspoon dried mint
- 1 teaspoon mango powder
- ½ teaspoon black salt
- ¼ teaspoon asafetida
- ½ teaspoon cayenne pepper
- ⅛ teaspoon powdered ginger
- ¾ teaspoon salt

Dry roast the cumin, pepper, and carom. Grind to a fine powder in a spice grinder with the mint and then mix with the other ingredients. Store the masala in an airtight container away from the light.

Sambar Powder

Type: South Indian
Speed: Fast
Notes: This is a kind of southern-style curry powder in which the coriander is dominant over the cumin. It also thickens a sauce, as it contains powdered dal.

- ¾ cup coriander seeds
- ¾ cup chana dal
- ⅓ cup grated desiccated coconut
- ¼ cup fenugreek seeds
- ¼ cup cumin seeds
- ¼ cup black mustard seeds
- 30 dried curry leaves

- 2 tablespoons urad dal
- 2 tablespoons black peppercorns
- 15 dry red chile peppers
- 3 tablespoons turmeric powder
- 1 tablespoon ginger powder
- 1 tablespoon asafetida

Dry roast the first 10 ingredients on low heat until they release their aroma, the chana dal starts to darken, and the coconut is a cinnamon color. Remove from the heat into a bowl, then add the turmeric, ginger, and asafetida. Grind in a spice grinder until you have a fine powder. Store in an airtight container away from sunlight.

Moong Dal Base

Type: Indian
Speed: Fast
Notes: Dal is an essential side dish in India and is flavored with a seemingly endless variety of ingredients. It can also be combined with vegetables for a filling main course. This recipe also works for red and yellow lentils as well as yellow split peas and yields about 4 cups.

- 1½ cups split moong dal
- 4½ cups water

- ¼ teaspoon turmeric
- 1 teaspoon salt

Check dal for foreign objects, like small stones; these are often in imported dal. Rinse the dal in several changes of water until the water runs clear. Drain. In a saucepan, combine the dal with the water and bring to a boil. I like to skim off any scum before adding the turmeric. After adding the turmeric, loosely cover pan with a lid and boil on medium-low heat for 30 minutes. If needed, you can add a little water if the dal starts to get too thick. It should be like a thick soup. Moong dal, red lentils, and split peas need no soak time for this dish, but the peas will need 45 minutes to cook. Add salt and whisk the dal with a fork to help break down any remaining whole peas.

This is a basic recipe. See page 67 for flavoring options.

North Indian Base Sauce

Type: North Indian
Speed: Less than an hour
Notes: Takeout and fast-food type Indian restaurants often rely on premade base sauces or at least partially prepared ingredient mixtures. Ostensibly, that is what a curry paste is. So a base sauce such as this would serve for serve for a vegetable "curry" and other dishes.

- ¼ cup oil
- 4 cups chopped onion (about 4 medium onions)
- 6 cloves garlic, chopped
- ¼ cup chopped fresh ginger
- 2 tablespoons ground coriander
- 1 tablespoon turmeric

- 1 tablespoon cayenne pepper
- 1 tablespoon ground fenugreek
- ½ teaspoon ground black pepper
- 1 tablespoon paprika
- 4 cups tomatoes, chopped
- 5 cups hot water
- 2 scant tablespoons salt

Heat the oil in a large saucepan. Add the onion and sauté on low to medium heat for 5 minutes. Add the garlic and ginger and fry, stirring to avoid burning, until the onions are a golden brown. Now add the coriander, turmeric, cayenne, fenugreek, black pepper, and paprika. Stir and be careful not to burn the spice mixture at this point. After a few seconds add the chopped tomatoes. Simmer on low heat for about 10 minutes, stirring occasionally. Add the hot water, cover, and cook over low heat for 20 minutes.

Let the saucepan cool a little, then process the sauce in batches in a blender to make a smooth sauce. Return it to the saucepan and bring to a boil. Add the salt and simmer for 10 minutes.

Cool and store for use in North Indian dishes.

Uses: Cabbage Curry (page 63), Cauliflower, Potato, and Methi Curry (page 97), Kofta Sauce (page 108), Potatoes and Cauliflower in Gravy (page 118), and Leftover Vegetable Korma (page 226).

Orange Flower Syrup

Type: Arabian
Speed: Very fast
Notes: Flavored syrups can be used for desserts, blended drinks, and additions to hot beverages.

- 3 cups sugar
- 1 cup water

- 2 tablespoons lemon juice
- 2 tablespoons orange flower water

Bring the sugar and water to a boil, reduce the heat, and simmer for 5 minutes, making sure all of the sugar has dissolved. Stir in the lemon juice and orange flower water. Set aside.

Uses: Donuts in Syrup (page 178) and Orange Slices in Syrup (page 184).

Option: For vanilla syrup, do as above but substitute a tablespoon of vanilla extract in place of the orange flower water.

Rutabaga Base Sauce

Type: Indian
Speed: Less than an hour
Notes: This curry is a good base sauce for barbecued sweet corn. You can substitute celery root or baked squash flesh for the rutabaga.

- 1 large rutabaga (about 1 pound), peeled and cut into small cubes
- 2 cups water
- 3 medium onions, peeled and chopped
- 2 cloves garlic, chopped
- 2 green chiles, chopped
- 1 tablespoon chopped fresh ginger
- ½ cup water
- 1 cup tomatoes, peeled and chopped
- 2 tablespoons coconut oil
- 2 tablespoons oil
- 1 teaspoon cumin seeds
- 2 whole cloves
- 2 cardamom pods

- 1 small stick cinnamon
- 1 tablespoon ground coriander seeds
- 3 medium tomatoes, chopped
- 1 teaspoon turmeric
- 1½ teaspoons salt
- 14-ounce can of coconut milk
- 2 tablespoons desiccated coconut
- 1 tablespoon urad dal
- 1 tablespoon sesame seeds
- ½ teaspoon garam masala
- 2 tablespoons oil
- 1 teaspoon black mustard
- 10 curry leaves
- 2 dry red chile peppers

Place the rutabaga in a large saucepan and cover with the 2 cups of water. Bring it to a boil, reduce the heat, and simmer for half an hour. If using baked squash, you can skip the simmering.

Meanwhile, put the onions, garlic, chiles, and ginger in a food processor with the ½ cup of water. Make a coarse paste. Set aside. Purée the tomatoes in the food processor. Set aside.

Heat 2 tablespoons of coconut oil and 2 tablespoons of vegetable oil in a large skillet. Add the cumin, cloves, cardamom, and cinnamon. As soon as they sizzle and the cumin turns a shade darker, add the onion paste. Fry the paste for about 10 minutes. It should darken slightly. Now add the coriander, tomatoes, turmeric, and salt.

Let the rutabaga cool a little, then purée along with its cooking liquid. Add it to the skillet along with the coconut milk and simmer for 5 minutes.

Dry roast the coconut, dal, and sesame seeds. Place in a spice grinder, grind to a fine powder, and stir into the skillet.

Mix in the garam masala.

Heat the remaining 2 tablespoons of oil in a small frying pan, add the black mustard seeds, and when they start popping add the curry leaves and red peppers. As soon as the peppers darken, tip the contents of the small frying pan into the skillet. Mix in. The sauce is now ready for sweet corn or koftas.

Uses: Brussels Sprouts in Rutabaga Sauce (page 62), Red Radishes in Rutabaga Sauce (page 77), and Instant Celery Root (or Rutabaga) Sambar (page 105)

White Nut Sauce

Type: Indian
Speed: Very fast
Notes: Using the base sauce technique, this sauce adds a heavy, rich taste and texture to the following dishes: Bananas in Nut Sauce (page 93), Fennel in Nut Sauce (page 102), Mushrooms in Nut Sauce (page 111), and Leftover Vegetable Korma (page 226).

- 3 tablespoons desiccated coconut
- 1 tablespoon coriander seeds
- 2 tablespoons white poppy seeds
- ½ cup cashews
- ¼ cup blanched almonds
- 1 cup plus ¼ cup water

Dry roast the coconut and coriander seeds on low heat in a frying pan until no white remains on the coconut and it is an even, light cinnamon color. Do not burn.

Grind the dry-roasted ingredients along with the poppy seeds in a spice grinder. In a blender, combine the ground mixture with the cashews, almonds, and a cup of water, and blend to make a smooth sauce. Pour into a container. Nuts are expensive, so use the extra ¼ cup of water to swill the remains of sauce from the blender into the container. Stir the sauce to make sure the extra water is blended. Store it in the refrigerator for use in the next couple of days or freeze in 1-cup containers for later use.

Eaters without Borders

A number of years ago, my friend Dee Dee and I went on one of our food pilgrimages, this time through Turkey and Syria to Lebanon. My Syrian entry visa, which I procured in Istanbul, required various communications and red tape between the British and Syrian embassies. It was all very proper.

The trip went splendidly with stops at the otherworldly Cappadocia and in Antakya, Homs, Hama, and Damascus. Finally in Beirut we indulged in the local fare: hummus, baba ghanoush, spinach pies, and of course pita bread. The most interesting example of pita bread we came across was a delivery service of sorts. A man cycled around carrying bread made with holes toward one edge so they could be hung from a wooden frame on his bike. The bread was tied on with strips of black plastic trash bags. He carried optional za'atar in a pouch that, upon request, he would sprinkle into the bread through a slit along the top. I stole the hole idea!

After a brief trip up the coast to the Byblos crusader castle, we returned to Beirut to find ourselves cut off by an Israeli blockade. Our original intent was to continue south, but the borders were closed and there were no available flights or ships out of the city. With limited options, and no local money, we returned to Syria. At the border we explained that our single entry visas had expired but needed to get back to Turkey. The border guard pointed to a guy in the middle of the road. Opening up his jacket as if to sell us stolen watches, the guy produced a bunch of stamps, almost filled 2 pages of our passports with them, charged us 30 U.S. dollars each, and we were on our way. No background check, no questions.

Breads & Pies

Bread, of some sort, has been enormously important among humans for thousands of years and takes a central role in the cuisines of many cultures. It is sometimes used in lieu of a spoon to eat dips and sauces, particularly in India. One of my favorite, easiest to make breads is Roti (page 219). I usually make enough dough for a couple of days and in minutes can produce hot flatbread. The downside to flatbread or griddle cakes for multiple guests is that someone has to guard the pan the whole time the production line is operating, but alternatively you can make enough to serve everyone, keeping them warm in the oven until they're all ready. Indian breakfast with flatbread and Chana Masala (page 98) is my favorite way to start the day and it's perfect for a light snack in the evening.

I have omitted tandoori breads because most people don't have access to a clay oven, and the famous tandori naan usually contains dairy in the form of yogurt. I've also omitted papadoms because they are inexpensive to buy and no one seems to make them at home these days. Instead I've offered several Indian breads of which some can be embellished with added ingredients. The Stuffed Paratha (page 219) is almost a meal on its own while the Chapati (page 32) is perhaps the easiest bread to make and can be used to sop up gravy or to fold around a little hot Indian food like a burrito.

Unlike the Indian flatbreads, the Lebanese and Moroccan breads (page 219) are leavened and are generally more filling. They come into their own with hot accompaniments like Harissa (page 155) where the greater bulk can combat the heat.

In Australia all manner of pies are sold in specialty shops or roadside wagons. Some of these outlets sell "vegetable curry" pies. You can make your own version by loading leftover Chana Masala (page 98) or Vegetable Curry Dal (page 235) into spinach pie dough to make individual pies. Bake and then freeze them for a quick snack for a journey.

Bread Topped with Za'atar

Type: Arabian
Preparation: Allow 1 to 2 hours for the dough to rise
Speed: About an hour after the rising time
Notes: This Lebanese bread is very filling and it is best eaten very fresh. Do not skimp on the kneading or the bread will be hard. While the dough is rising, you will have time to attend to other dishes.

- ½ teaspoon active yeast
- ½ teaspoon sugar
- 3 tablespoons warm water
- 3 cups all-purpose flour
- ½ teaspoon salt
- 1 cup warm water
- 2 tablespoons za'atar
- 2 tablespoons olive oil

Activate the yeast in a small bowl by mixing it with sugar and 3 tablespoons of warm water. While the yeast mixture stands, combine the flour and salt in a large bowl. Once the yeast mixture has foamed up, dilute it with a cup of warm water, then add it to the bowl of flour and stir in. Work the mixture for 10 minutes with your hands, kneading on a floured surface until you have rubbery dough. Place the dough in a lightly oiled bowl and keep covered with cheesecloth or a towel in a warm place until it rises to almost twice its original size. This will take more than an hour. Punch the dough down, form it into a ball, and set aside under the towel for 10 more minutes.

Roll the dough out to form four flat oval loaves, around ¾ inch thick. Let them stand covered with a slightly damp cloth for half an hour. Preheat the oven to 400°F and then make a paste with the za'atar and oil. Lightly coat the top of each loaf with the za'atar paste before baking them for around 20 minutes. A pizza stone can help to get a crusty bottom. I have a convection oven, which cooks very fast, so cooking times may vary a little depending on your oven.

Chapati

Type: Indian
Speed: Very fast
Notes: In India, bread is often used instead of cutlery to eat curry sauce. The chapati is the simplest of Indian breads—thin and not highly flavored, making it perfect for preserving the flavor of the dish. You can also make chapatis with half all-purpose and half flax flour.

- 1½ cups whole-wheat flour
- ½ cup warm water
- Pinch of salt
- 1 tablespoon oil

Mix the flour, water, and salt in a food processor until you have an elastic dough. Add the oil and process until the oil is fully absorbed. Finish kneading by hand to form a smooth, pliable dough.

Dust your work surface with a little flour. Divide the dough into 8 balls and keep them under plastic wrap until you are ready for them. Heat the griddle or pancake pan on high.

Roll the first chapati very thin. You do not need any oil on the griddle or pan. Lay the chapati on the hot surface and cook until it starts to form dark patches underneath. Flip it over and cook the other side. Repeat this process until all of the chapatis are made. Serve them immediately or place them in a shallow bowl and cover with a damp cloth in a warm oven until needed. You can also revive chapatis by lightly brushing them with oil and reheating on the griddle.

Flax Roti

Type: Indian
Preparation: Grind flax seeds to a meal in a spice grinder
Speed: Fast

Notes: This easy-to-make flatbread goes with almost any Indian dish and substitutes for a fork or spoon. I find that whole-wheat roti is often dry, but this flax seed adaptation has that extra nutty flavor and maintains a nice moist finish.

- 3 cups all-purpose flour
- ½ cup ground flax seed
- ½ teaspoon salt
- ½ teaspoon cayenne pepper
- 1 tablespoon nigella seeds
- 1¼ cups warm water

Mix all the dry ingredients in a bowl, then add the water and form the dough. Turn onto a floured work surface and knead hard for about 5 minutes. The dough should now be somewhat elastic. Place a large frying pan over high heat. The type of pan will make a great difference to the finished bread. In a heavy nonstick pan, it is sometimes hard to get the desired finish because it can dry out the dough. I prefer the type of pan with raised ridges (the surface looks a little like a phonograph record). Either way, preheat the pan in order to sear the bread nicely.

Keep the work surface lightly floured and roll out a portion of dough. The size depends on whether you are making about 10 small pieces or about 6 large ones. Roll the dough into a rough circle with a rolling pin, adding a little more flour as needed. Lay it into the frying pan. When the bread begins to smoke— after a couple of minutes—flip it. There should be small patches where the bread is starting to darken. After doing both sides, tease the bread over the open flame using tongs. (If you have an electric cook top you will be unable to get that burnt finish.) This stage finishes any doughy creases or parts not cooked. Serve immediately.

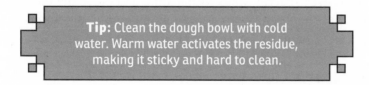

Tip: Clean the dough bowl with cold water. Warm water activates the residue, making it sticky and hard to clean.

Moroccan Bread

Type: North African
Preparation: Allow about 1½ hours and another hour for rising
Speed: About 20 minutes after the rising times
Notes: Moroccan bread would not look out of place in any Western bakery. It is not particularly exotic, but it is central to the cuisine. Urban families transport bread dough to communal ovens on wooden trays most often on the heads of the children. Some of these bakeries are quite cavernous, where the individually marked trays sit on the floor awaiting oven space. The dough is then sent into the large brick oven on a flat wooden shovel. Once baked it is ready to be retrieved by the child courier. This seems almost ritualistic and shows the importance of bread to Moroccan cuisine. The loaves are generally a round, flattish dome shape. Anise seeds are a common addition, but optional.

- 3 cups all-purpose flour
- 1 cup whole-wheat flour
- 1 teaspoon anise seeds
- 1 tablespoon salt
- 1 tablespoon active yeast
- 1 teaspoon sugar
- ¼ cup lukewarm water
- 1½ cups warm water
- A little olive oil
- A little cornmeal

In a bowl, mix the flours, anise, and salt. Proof the yeast in a small bowl with the sugar and lukewarm water for 4 minutes. Stir the mixture into the 1½ cups of warm water, then add it to the flour and form a ball with your hands. Dust a surface with a little flour and knead for 10 minutes until you have a nice elastic dough.

Lightly oil a bowl and place the dough in. Cover with plastic wrap. Let the bowl sit for at least 1½ hours in a warm place. By this time the dough should have more than doubled in size. Knock down the dough and form into one or two flattish loaves. Sprinkle a baking tray with the cornmeal and place the dough on it. Cover with a clean, damp cloth for an hour to re-rise.

Preheat the oven to 400°F.

Prick the loaves several times with a knife and place the bakingtray in the oven. I often put the dough onto a pizza stone, and I sometimes put a small ovenproof bowl of water in the oven to keep the bread moist. Bake for about 45 minutes.

Like most bread, it is best eaten warm, right out of the oven.

Pita Bread

Type: Arabian
Preparation: Allow a couple of hours rising time
Speed: About 30 minutes after the rising time
Notes: Is it worth making your own pita bread? If you have a convenient source of fresh, good-quality authentic pita then perhaps not, but if all you have in your neighborhood is the dry supermarket variety then certainly it is.

- ½ teaspoon sugar
- ¼ ounce packet of dried yeast
- 1½ cups warm water
- 3 cups all-purpose flour
- 1 cup whole-wheat flour
- 1 teaspoon salt
- ½ teaspoon vegetable oil

Mix the sugar and yeast into half a cup of the warm water and let it stand for a few minutes.

Meanwhile, mix the flours, salt, and oil in a large bowl. Now add the rest of the warm water and the yeast water. Work the mixture into a dough with your hands.

Knead the dough on a clean surface, lightly dusted with flour. After about 10 minutes put the dough into a lightly oiled bowl and cover with a damp towel Allow it to stand in a warm area for a couple of hours until it doubles in size.

Knead the dough again to reduce its size and divide it into 8 even-sized balls. Place the balls on a lightly dusted work surface and cover them with plastic wrap. Preheat the oven to 475°F with a metal baking tray inside. Roll out a couple of balls into 8-inch diameter, flat circles. Place them on the tray and bake for a couple of minutes. The bread should not be crisped but remain soft. Sometimes they part and blow up like a balloon.

Eat them warm or freeze for later use.

> **Tip:** In the winter I warm the oven, switch off the heat, and leave the bowl inside covered with a clean tea towel. It will take a couple of hours for the dough to rise. During that time you can briefly turn the heat on to keep the oven warm, but at no time let the oven get hot, only warm.

Poori

Breads
& Pies

Type: Indian
Preparation: You can make the dough in advance
Speed: Fast
Notes: Pooris are best served straight from the stove to the plate, so leave the final stage of poori preparation until you've finished all the other dishes.

- 1½ cups all-purpose flour
- 1½ cups whole-wheat flour
- ½ teaspoon ground black pepper
- ½ teaspoon salt
- 3 tablespoons oil
- 1 cup water
- Oil for frying

Mix the flours, pepper, salt, and oil in a bowl. Pour in the water and knead out the dough on a lightly floured surface. Work for 10 minutes, then wrap in plastic wrap and refrigerate until needed.

Remove the dough from the refrigerator and knead for a couple of minutes to soften. Divide into 16 balls and cover with plastic wrap. On a floured surface, roll out each ball into a flat, round sheet about 7 inches in diameter. To fry each piece of bread you will need a frying pan, oil about 1 inch deep, and a spatula (or wooden tongs, which I use).

Heat the oil until very hot, almost smoking, then carefully lower the first piece slowly in and use your utensil to hold it down. It will take only a few seconds to fry one side. Carefully turn the bread over and fry the second side. The finish should be light golden and the bread may blow up like a balloon. Be careful not to puncture the ballooned bread while it is in the oil. Lift the bread out and shake excess oil back into the pan. Lay the bread on a plate lined with a paper towel while you finish enough to serve. You can knock down the bread now to release the air if you wish.

Spinach Pies

Type: Lebanese
Preparation: Defrost the spinach. Allow 1 to 2 hours for the dough to rise
Speed: A little over an hour after the rising time
Notes: I like these pies best cold (cool, then refrigerate in a plastic container) but they can also be eaten hot.

- 1 pound frozen spinach
- 1 teaspoon active yeast
- ½ teaspoon sugar
- 3 tablespoons plus 1 cup warm water
- 2½ cups all-purpose flour
- 1 teaspoon salt
- 3 tablespoons olive oil

- 2 tablespoons lemon juice
- 2 tablespoons pine nuts
- 1 small onion, diced
- ¼ small Preserved Lemon (page 165), finely chopped
- 1½ teaspoons salt
- Za'atar

Place the spinach in a bowl to defrost.

In a cup, stir the active yeast and sugar into the 3 tablespoons warm water. Wait until the yeast expands, about 4 or 5 minutes, and mix into the rest of the water. Mix the flour and salt in a bowl, add the yeast water, and form it with your hands until you have dough. Move the dough onto your floured work surface and knead for 10 minutes, adding a little flour to the surface as you need it. Clean the bowl using cold water, dry, and grease it with a little olive oil. Make a ball out of the dough and place it in the bowl. Cover with a clean tea towel and place it in a warm place until it has risen to around twice its size. Knead the dough again for a couple of minutes, then let it stand covered with plastic wrap.

Preheat the oven to 385°F.

Once the spinach has defrosted, squeeze it with your hands in batches to remove as much excess water as you can and return to the bowl. Mix in the olive oil, lemon juice, pine nuts, onion, preserved lemon, and 1½ teaspoons of salt. Toss with your hands until all the ingredients are evenly distributed.

Decide the size, number, and shape of the pies you wish to make. Work the dough and coat with a little olive oil. To make one big pie, use a circular baking tray and tease out the dough like a pizza, overlapping the edges enough to make a top for the pie. Put the entire filling in. Level off and fold the edges over until they meet in the center. Pinch the edges together to seal the pie.

You can make 4 smaller pies in a similar manner using a flat baking tray, or 8 individual pies. In each case divide the filling accordingly.

Brush the top of the pies with olive oil and sprinkle a wisp of za'atar on each. (This stage is optional.) Place the pies in the oven until they start to go golden brown on top: about 40 minutes for the larger pies, perhaps a little less for the small ones.

Stuffed Paratha

Type: Indian
Preparation: Cook mashed potatoes and defrost peas
Speed: About an hour
Notes: These stuffed flatbreads should be light and a little flakey. Use top-quality, finely milled whole-wheat flour. Stuffed parathas are perfect with a light soup and some sweet chutney.

- 2 cups whole-wheat flour
- 1 cup all-purpose flour
- 1 teaspoon salt
- 1 cup warm water
- ¼ cup plus 1 tablespoon oil
- 1 tablespoon finely chopped fresh ginger
- 1 small green chile, seeded and finely chopped

- 1 teaspoon carom seeds
- 1 teaspoon cumin seeds
- ¼ teaspoon turmeric
- ½ teaspoon salt
- 1 tablespoon ground coriander
- 1 teaspoon mango powder
- 2 cups coarsely mashed potato
- ¼ cup frozen peas, defrosted

Combine the flours and salt in a food processor. Then add the water followed by the ¼ cup of oil. Process until an elastic dough forms, about 3 minutes. Remove the dough from the processor and knead with your hands for 2 minutes. Let it rest in a bowl, covered with a clean tea towel, for half an hour.

Heat the tablespoon of oil in an iron skillet and add the ginger, chile, carom, and cumin seeds. After a few seconds of stirring, add the turmeric, salt, coriander, and mango powder. Stir thoroughly, then add the potato. Mix until the spices are evenly distributed, then fold in the peas. Mix and stand to the side to cool.

Divide the dough into 8 balls. Roll one out to about 6 inches in diameter. Put ⅛ of the filling in the center. Fold the sides over, covering and sealing the filling. Roll out the filled dough again until it is about 8 or 9 inches. Heat the frying pan and put in the bread. Flip it when it starts to cook. Make sure you don't burn it. Brush the cooked side with oil while the other side cooks, flip again and brush the second side. The bread will cook quickly, so be vigilant.

Vegetable Samosas

Type: Indian
Preparation: You can make the pastry dough ahead of time
Speed: A couple of hours, depending on your skill level
Notes: Samosas are the perfect finger food served with tamarind dipping sauce. In India you can find them sizzling in the giant iron skillets of the street vendors. This recipe uses coriander in three ways at three different stages of cooking: fresh (cilantro), whole, and ground. Makes 16 samosas.

- 1½ cups all-purpose flour
- ½ teaspoon salt
- ¼ cup warm water

- 4 tablespoons margarine, cut into 1-inch cubes

- 2 pounds potatoes, peeled and cut into ½-inch cubes
- 2 to 4 hot chiles
- 1 tablespoon finely chopped fresh ginger
- 1 large onion, chopped
- 2 tablespoons fresh cilantro, chopped
- ¼ cup oil

- 1 teaspoon coriander seeds
- 1 teaspoon cumin seeds
- 1 cup frozen peas, defrosted
- 1 teaspoon ground cumin
- 1 teaspoon ground coriander
- 2 teaspoons mango powder
- 1 teaspoon salt
- 1 teaspoon garam masala
- ¼ cup water

- Extra dusting flour
- A bowl of water

- Oil for deep frying

In a food processor, combine the flour, salt, and margarine. Run the processor until the margarine is fully integrated into the flour. Add the water, slowly running the processor until the dough forms into a ball or, depending on the machine, forms into doughy crumbs. You may need a couple of extra tablespoons of water. Remove the dough from the machine, form into a ball, and knead for 5 minutes. Wrap the dough in plastic wrap and refrigerate while you make the filling.

Bring a large saucepan of salt water to a boil and add the potato. Return to a boil and cook for about 5 minutes. You want the potatoes to be cooked through but firm. You can shock them with cold water to prevent them cooking further if you need to. Drain and set aside.

While the potatoes are cooking, make a paste out of the chiles (2 for mild, more for spicy), ginger, onion, and cilantro in the food processor. Heat the oil in a large skillet and add the coriander and cumin seeds. Fry until they are darker, then add the onion paste from the processor. Keep stirring to prevent it from burning for about 5 minutes. Add the peas and drained potatoes, tossing until they are coated with the onion mixture. Add the cumin, coriander, mango powder, salt, and garam masala. Mix in to coat the potatoes with spice. Add water and cover on low heat for 3 minutes. Transfer to a bowl and allow to cool for a few minutes.

The dough should have stayed in the refrigerator for about an hour. Take it out and soften it up by kneading for a few minutes. Divide it into 8 even balls and roll in your hands until smooth. Lay each out on the work surface and cover with plastic wrap. Pour oil into a saucepan to a depth of around 5 inches. Heat until a nip of dough will sizzle if dropped in. Put a small bowl of water next to the cook top and dust a work surface with flour. Roll out the first ball until it's about a 7-inch even circle. Cut the circle in half. Taking one half, fold it around to make something like a mini ice cream cone. Wet one edge with the water and press the edges firmly together. Now you have a cone. Take a spoonful of the filling and fill the cone not quite to the top. You need enough edge left to fold one edge over the filling. Again, wet it, then close it with the other edge like sealing an envelope. Carefully lower the samosa into the hot oil. It should sizzle, but not explosively. While it fries, go on to the second half of the ball. Work through the 8 balls, each making 2 samosas, until you are finished. When each samosa reaches a golden brown spoon it onto a plate. You will find that as you proceed the samosas will generally be a little darker. If you are making them to freeze for later use, it's a good idea to keep them a little on the light side so when you reheat them you have a little leeway.

Serve hot with Tamarind Dipping Sauce (page 168).

Tip: Samosas are a perfect candidate for freezing. I recommend that if you are committed to making them, you might as well make a double or triple batch and freeze some for later.

Dem Bones, Dem Bones . . .

I remember one particular incident, perhaps in Slovakia, where a waitress, reasonably articulate in the English language, assured me that the soup was vegetarian. The soup was the only hope because even the bread was flecked with ham. Primed for misunderstanding, I persevered for as long as I dared asking about every ingredient. No, she assured me, there is no meat or meat stock whatsoever in the soup. Reluctantly, I ordered the soup but made one last stealthy probe. "How do you make the soup?" I asked non-accusingly. "Well, we start by boiling bones in a large pot . . ." Thus has been our lot, particularly outside of large cities, at least until recent years and the arrival of more ethnic eateries.

Soups

Indians make "soup" with every thickness you could want, from the thin but fiery pepper water to heavy stews and dals. I'm particularly fond of the thin south Indian rasam, Tomato (page 219), Onion (page 219), and Pepper Broth (page 233).

I developed the Apple Soup (page 219) version of rasam using the fruit on my land near Quedlinburg in Germany. Alf, the resident horse, seemed indifferent to the many apple trees, but I soon realized he was adept at identifying and eating only the sweetest harvest. Rasam usually has a sour element—lemon, tomato, tamarind, etc.—so the trees that Alf says nay to, often the more ancient trees, are a perfect source for this dish. At the height of the summer a scorching rasam is a grand way to combat the heat without being too filling.

I first had Jerusalem Artichoke Soup (page 48) back in the 1970s at David's house. Sunchokes (Jerusalem artichokes) are not related to artichokes but are a variety of sunflower. They used to be a little hard to find, but seem to be getting more popular, if expensive. However, they grow easily, so that might be an option. This soup couldn't be easier to make and its creaminess defies its meager ingredients.

For the Butternut Squash (page 46) recipe it is a good idea to have previously baked the squash (see Ganging Up on page 15). You can also try other varieties for a change of pace. I often substitute acorn squash and have also used turban squash—both work fine. In this regard, shopping for what is on sale and preparing it on the barbecue for later use maximizes your savings.

In the Recycled section
Nettle Soup (page 231)
Pepper Broth (page 233)

Apple Soup

Type: Indian
Speed: A little over an hour
Notes: This is a spicy soup and is meant to be quite thin.

- ¼ cup moong dal
- 2 cups water
- ½ teaspoon turmeric
- ¼ teaspoon tamarind concentrate
- 2 tablespoons desiccated coconut
- 3 tablespoons oil
- 1½ teaspoons black mustard seed
- 1½ teaspoons cumin seeds
- ½ teaspoon asafetida
- 1 small cinnamon stick

- 6 curry leaves
- 3 green chiles, chopped
- 1 teaspoon ground black pepper
- 1 tablespoon chopped ginger
- 2 cooking apples, peeled, cored, and chopped into ½-inch cubes.
- 1 cup water
- 1 tablespoon salt
- Fresh cilantro for garnish

Rinse the dal in several changes of water, drain, then add 2 cups of water, the turmeric, and tamarind. Bring it to a boil, cover, and simmer on low heat until the dal is fully cooked and smooth, about an hour. Add more water as needed and do not let the pan dry out. Dry roast the coconut to an even cinnamon color, grind it to a powder in a spice grinder, and then mix it into the dal and set aside off the heat.

In a large skillet, heat the oil, then add the mustard and cumin. As the mustard seeds start to pop, add the asafetida, cinnamon, and curry leaves. Turn heat to low. Add the chiles, pepper, ginger, and apple. Stir to coat in oil and fry for 2 minutes, and then add a cup of water and the salt. Cook for another 5 minutes before pouring the contents into the dal. Add another 2½ cups of water and bring the pot back to a boil. Serve hot, garnished with a few cilantro leaves.

Butternut Squash Soup

Type: North African
Preparation: You can use prebaked squash from the barbecue. If you are starting from scratch, add time to bake a squash. You will also need 5 cups of vegetable stock (page 17).
Speed: About 30 minutes using preprepared elements

Soups

- ½ cup red lentils
- 5 cups vegetable stock (page 17)
- 2 tablespoons olive oil
- 1 large onion, chopped
- 2½ cups butternut squash pulp (page 15)
- ½ teaspoon Harissa (page 155) or cayenne pepper
- ¼ Preserved Lemon (page 165) (or 1 tablespoon lemon juice)
- 1½ teaspoon salt
- ¼ teaspoon ground black pepper
- Finely chopped lovage or cilantro leaves for garnish

Rinse the lentils until the water runs clear. Drain, then put them into a large saucepan with the vegetable stock and bring to a boil. Reduce to low heat and cover, simmering for about 20 minutes. Heat the oil in a frying pan and fry the onion until it is golden brown, about 5 minutes.

In a food processor, process, in batches if necessary, the fried onion, cooked lentils, squash, harissa, lemon, and salt. Return the soup to the saucepan and bring it to a boil. Turn down the heat to a simmer and fold in the black pepper.

Serve in small bowls as a starter, garnished with the fresh herbs.

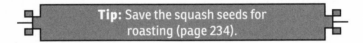

Tip: Save the squash seeds for roasting (page 234).

Cashew Soup

Type: Indian
Speed: About an hour
Notes: This soup is extremely rich and therefore should be served in small bowls. It also thickens easily as it stands, so serve it straight from the cook top. When it is made in advance it might be a good idea to thin it out with a little additional water.

- ¼ cup urad dal
- 4 cups water
- 6 ounces raw cashews
- ¼ cup white poppy seeds, ground to a powder
- 2 tablespoons oil
- 1 teaspoon black mustard seeds
- 1 tablespoon sesame seeds
- 2 cloves garlic, chopped
- 4 large dry red chiles, broken into pieces
- 8 curry leaves
- 1½ teaspoon salt
- Dry-roasted cashews, for garnish

Rinse the dal until the water runs clear and bring to a boil with 2 cups of water in a saucepan. Cover and simmer until the dal is mushy, about 35 minutes. Let the pan cool a little. In a blender, blend the cashews, ground poppy seeds, and another cup of water until you have a smooth paste. Add the dal broth and another cup of water to the blender and blend until it is smooth. (You may need to do this in batches.) Return the soup to a saucepan. Heat the oil in a skillet and add the mustard and sesame seeds. As soon as the mustard seeds start to pop, add the garlic, chiles, and curry leaves. Put the fried ingredients into the pot, add the salt and simmer for 10 minutes. Add some more water if the soup gets too stiff, but it should remain quite thick. Serve in small bowls and garnish with dry-roasted cashews.

Jerusalem Artichoke Soup

Type: Arabian
Preparation: You will need vegetable stock (page 17)
Speed: About 45 minutes (mostly peeling time)
Notes: Jerusalem artichokes, also known as sunchokes, are not actually related to artichokes. They make a creamy and rich soup with very little added, making this just about the simplest recipe I know.

Soups

- 1 pound Jerusalem artichokes
- 4 cups vegetable stock (page 17)
- ½ teaspoon salt
- Pinch of ground black pepper

Carefully peel the Jerusalem artichokes retaining as much flesh as possible. As you do this, immediately place the artichokes in a bowl of water to prevent discoloration. You should have around 12 ounces once the peels are discarded.

Bring the vegetable stock and salt to a boil and add the artichokes. Boil for about 15 minutes on medium-low heat. Let cool a little and put into a blender. Blend to a smooth soup. Fold in a little pepper, reheat, and serve hot.

Lentil Soup

Type: Arabian
Preparation: You will need vegetable stock (page 17)
Speed: About 1½ hours, but you will have time to do other things while it's cooking
Notes: This soup is both filling and inexpensive. You can substitute half a finely chopped Preserved Lemon (page 165) for the rhubarb.

- ⅓ cup olive oil
- 2 large onions, chopped
- 1½ cups water
- 2 cups lentils
- 12 cups vegetable stock (page 17)
- ¼ cup rice
- ½ teaspoon caraway seeds
- ½ teaspoon dill seeds
- 4 stalks rhubarb
- ¼ teaspoon freshly ground black pepper

- 2 tablespoons tomato paste
- 2 large tomatoes, chopped
- 1 teaspoon turmeric
- 1 tablespoon salt
- ¼ teaspoon Harissa (optional, page 155)
- ¼ cup olive oil
- 1 tablespoon fresh parsley, diced
- 4 cloves garlic, chopped

Fry the onions in the olive oil in a saucepan until dark golden brown. Add 1½ cups of water and continue to heat until most of the water is absorbed into the onions and you are left with a mush. Rinse the lentils in cold water, then add to the pan with the stock and rice. Bring the pan to a boil, then simmer until lentils are soft, about 45 minutes.

Dry roast the whole caraway and dill seeds, then grind them in a spice grinder. Set aside. The soup should now be thick—like porridge—but you may have to add more water along the way and stir from time to time to prevent sticking. Strip the outer skin from the rhubarb, cut into ¾-inch pieces. Add them to the soup along with the pepper, roasted caraway and dill powder, tomato paste, tomatoes, turmeric, salt, and Harissa. Then cook for about 15 more minutes, adding water as needed.

Heat the olive oil in a small saucepan and fry the parsley and garlic for a few seconds. Pour this over the soup and stir in. Serve hot.

Onion Rasam

Type: South Indian
Speed: About an hour

- 1 cup toor dal
- 3½ cups water
- ¼ teaspoon turmeric
- 1½ teaspoon salt
- ¼ teaspoon tamarind concentrate
- 1 tomato, chopped
- 2 hot chiles, finely chopped
- 1 teaspoon desiccated coconut
- 1 teaspoon coriander seeds
- 1 teaspoon ground black pepper
- 1 large onion, finely sliced

- 3 cups water
- 3 tablespoons oil
- 1 teaspoon black mustard seeds
- ½ teaspoon cumin seeds
- ½ teaspoon fenugreek seeds
- ½ teaspoon asafetida
- 25 curry leaves
- 1 tablespoon lemon juice
- 1 tablespoon fresh cilantro, chopped

Rinse the dal until the water runs clear. Drain, then bring the dal to a boil in a saucepan with 3½ cups of water and the turmeric. Reduce to low heat and cover with the lid ajar and simmer for half an hour.

Dry roast the coconut and coriander until it is an even cinnamon color, then grind to a powder in a spice grinder.

Use a potato masher to crush the dal, then add the salt, tamarind, tomato, chiles, coconut-coriander mixture, pepper, onion, and extra water. Cook for another 20 minutes. Heat the oil over a medium heat in a small frying pan, then add the black mustard seeds. Once the seeds start to pop, add the cumin and fenugreek seeds. Stir, then after a few seconds add the asafetida. Let it sizzle, then add the curry leaves. Stir and let the leaves crackle, then pour the contents onto the dal. Fold the ingredients together, add the lemon juice, and serve with a sprinkle of chopped cilantro.

Tomato Rasam

Type: South Indian
Speed: About an hour
Notes: Rasam is a thin, southern Indian soup eaten with rice or alone. It can be made using rasam powder. In this recipe I build the soup from scratch.

- 3 tablespoons red lentils (masoor dal)
- 1 cup water
- ½ teaspoon turmeric
- 3 large tomatoes, finely chopped
- ¼ teaspoon tamarind concentrate
- 3 tablespoons oil
- 1 teaspoon black mustard seeds

- ½ teaspoon cumin seeds
- ½ teaspoon asafetida
- 2 dry red chiles
- 8 curry leaves
- 3 cloves garlic, minced
- 2 cups water
- 1 teaspoon salt
- Fresh cilantro leaves for garnish

Soups

Rinse the dal until the water runs clear. Then bring it to a boil with the turmeric in a saucepan with 1 cup of water. Reduce the heat and simmer on low for about 20 minutes until the dal is mushy. Do not let the pan dry out. Add the tomatoes and tamarind concentrate. Cover and simmer on low heat, adding a little water if needed.

Heat the oil in a skillet, then add the mustard and cumin seeds. When the mustard seeds start to pop, add the asafetida, chile peppers, curry leaves, and garlic. Stir until the peppers turn dark, but be careful not to burn the garlic. Scrape the fried spices into the saucepan and add 2 more cups of water and the salt. Simmer until the tomato is completely absorbed into the soup.

Transfer to bowls and garnish with the cilantro.

For starters

In the early '70s I studied classic guitar in Leicester for a number of years. Lessons there, while perhaps not dreaded, were a chore. Things normally ran a little late, so one sat in the dim corridor next to the grandfather clock listening to the cat-like shrieks of the kid before grinding a violin. Once in the music room, you were greeted by an overwhelming smell of mangy dogs. My tutor, who was quite a ripe age, sat sometimes at the piano and sometimes on a chair listening while the homework was played. Often after a few bars her head seemed to drop on the verge of nodding off, but any transgression would bring her back to life like smelling salts. The agenda, at least for her, seemed to be entrance into Leicester Festival of Music and Dramatic Art. My agenda was a little less grandiose; I just wanted to play the music of Bach. Still, after going through the appropriate grades, it was to the Festival I went in 1975 and 1976 to play Bach.

Over the previous couple of years, I'd been continually slapped on the knee and chided about my left hand position, and finally in '76 I was told I'd better choose between classical or that pop music stuff. Not much of a choice, really, because I was not nearly good enough to do anything meaningful on classical guitar.

Leicester already had one of Europe's largest Indian communities, in no small part due to the 1947 partition of India and subsequent British Nationality Act 1948. Further, tens of thousands of East African Asians fled to Leicester in the early 1970s as a result of the Idi Amin–led "Africanization" policies in East Africa. The city boasted numerous restaurants and takeout storefronts decades before most of England embraced the cuisine.

Newly mobile with my grey minivan, I could now stop for samosas and dipping sauce after class on the return drive to our rural village, which was entirely devoid of any Indian population.

I think this was the beginning of my love for Indian food, and certainly a new world of vegetarian possibilities presented itself. Many Hindus, traditionally, complied with 100 percent meat-free meals, and thus I became emboldened to explore the cuisine ever deeper.

Starters & Side Dishes

Starters and side dishes will add some zing to a meal, but it's not always necessary to toil over every element of a dinner party to impress. One system I use all the time is to offset certain dishes by a few days and resurrect them, perhaps slightly modified as a side dish. For example, a moong dal might be the main course for a light lunch on Monday, then reappear from the freezer on Friday refreshed by tempering with hot oil and spices.

Sometimes a meal, particularly a party buffet, has no "main course." Instead, the table is a spread of a variety of dishes. In this chapter the starters and side dishes can certainly be served en masse as a buffet or presented in a more traditional style in successive courses. It really doesn't matter.

A side dish is a great opportunity to flex your artistic muscle in the presentation. The portions are usually smaller, allowing for a decorative serving dish or plate to stand out. Whether it's "hummus art" (page 71) or Pine Nut Pâté (page 75) in an attractive bowl, this is a chance to wow. A small portion of Fenugreek Purée (page 66) in a wide-rimmed dish holding strips of Roti (page 33) will get a great response. This attention to detail really enhances the eating experience, and your guests are far more likely to savor the food and appreciate your efforts.

Another technique I use is to combine elements together, for instance serving a Flavored Moong Dal (page 67) in a bowl set at the center of a large plate of Split Pea Koftas (page 85), or surrounding the colorful Stuffed Peppers (page 87) with something like Spicy Fava Bean Salad (page 145) from the salad section.

In the Recycled section
Besan Scramble (page 222)
Nettle Saag (page 230)
Pakoras (page 232)
Roasted Squash/Pumpkin Seeds (page 234)
Watermelon Rind Bharta (page 237)

Apple Curry

Type: Indian
Speed: About 30 minutes
Notes: This a rich, sweet dish, best served with basmati rice and a lime pickle.

- ¼ cup oil
- 1 large onion, chopped
- ½ teaspoon cumin seeds
- ½ teaspoon ground coriander
- ½ teaspoon cayenne pepper
- 2 bay leaves
- 8 dates, pitted and chopped

- ¼ teaspoon turmeric
- ½ teaspoon salt
- 1 teaspoon mango powder
- 2 large green apples
- 3 ounces raw cashews
- ½ cup water
- ½ teaspoon garam masala

Starters & Side Dishes

Heat oil in a large saucepan and add the onion and cumin. Fry, stirring until the onions are golden brown. Turn the heat to low, then add the coriander, cayenne, and bay leaves. Stir and add the dates, turmeric, salt, and mango powder. Peel and core the apples, chop them into ½-inch chunks, and stir them into the saucepan. In a food processor, blend the nuts in the water until you have a smooth paste. Add to the pan, cover, and steam for 5 minutes or until the apple is cooked but not mushy. Fold in the garam masala and serve hot in a shallow dish.

Baba Ghanoush

Type: Lebanese
Preparation: You will need fire-roasted eggplant (page 15)
Speed: Fast
Notes: This version of baba ghanoush is light and sweet, using charcoal-grilled eggplant.

- 2 large cloves garlic
- ½ cup tahini
- 2 medium lemons, juiced
- ¼ Preserved Lemon (page 165) (optional)
- 1 teaspoon salt
- 2 tablespoons pine nuts

- 1½ cups fire-roasted eggplant pulp (about 3 large eggplants)
- Olive oil
- Dash of paprika
- Seeds from ½ medium-sized pomegranate (option A)
- Hearts from 3 artichokes (option B)

Place the garlic, tahini, lemon juice, preserved lemon, and salt into a food processor and blend until no lumps of garlic remain. For instructions on roasting eggplant, see page 15. Add the eggplant pulp and blend to a paste either with a little texture or smooth, depending on your preference. Taste for saltiness and adjust if needed.

Put the paste onto a deep plate and spread out to about 2 inches from the edge. Make a bowl-shaped depression into the baba ghanoush and pour in about ¼ cup of olive oil, making a reservoir. Sprinkle on the pine nuts and dress with a flair of paprika.

Options

A. To garnish the baba ghanoush more formally, place it into a shallow bowl and smooth and seal with olive oil using the back of a spoon. Make a crosshatch pattern with paprika and put pine nuts or halved olives where the lines cross. Circle the perimeter with pomegranate seeds.

B. Pair the baba ghanoush with artichoke hearts. Wash the artichokes, put them in a large saucepan, and barely cover with water. Add 2 teaspoons of salt and bring to a boil. Cover and simmer until the artichokes are cooked but not mushy. Let them cool and then remove the leaves. Dress the hearts by removing the top fibers (the choke). Cut the hearts in half and rub them with olive oil. Place the artichoke heart halves around the space at the edge of the plate.

Besan Pancakes

Type: Indian
Preparation: Precook a potato
Speed: Fast
Notes: Serve these spicy Indian pancakes with a sweet chutney as a light meal or at breakfast.

- 1 cup besan (chickpea flour)
- ½ cup cold water
- 1 tablespoon finely chopped ginger
- 1 green chile, finely chopped
- ½ teaspoon salt
- ¼ teaspoon asafetida
- 1 cooked potato, coarsely mashed
- Oil for frying

Mix the besan and water in a bowl until you have a smooth batter with no lumps. Mix in the remaining ingredients thoroughly (except the oil). Heat a couple of tablespoons of oil in a nonstick frying pan. Pour in enough batter to make the desired size and tease it out to a round pancake with the back of a spoon. Open up a small coin-sized hole in the center and scoop a little oil into the middle. This helps prevent the center from sticking and makes an attractive donut-shaped pancake. Flip and fry the second side. It should be golden with patches of brown. The second side will have firmed a little, so you can press down with a spatula to make better contact. You may have to add a little more oil.

Move the pancakes to a plate and serve with sweet chutney.

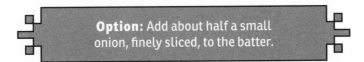

Option: Add about half a small onion, finely sliced, to the batter.

Bitter Melons with Onion

Type: Indian
Preparation: 1½ hours soaking
Speed: About 30 minutes
Notes: If you are new to Indian food and to bitter melon, this might not be the place to start. I love this vegetable but fear a newcomer might start with this recipe and go no further. It is an acquired taste, and with the help of sweet chutney such as Fruit and Nut (page 154), I think you might return to it. There are two types of bitter melon normally available in Western markets: the smoother light-green Chinese variety and the darker Indian type with its more textured skin. Indian bitter melon is harder to find but worth the search for its stronger and indeed more bitter taste. If you elect to grow your own bitter melons, note that the vine too can be cooked and eaten, usually with other greens like collards or kale. Here the bitterness is checked by the use of salt to draw out the bitter juice, revealing a much-underrated vegetable in the West.

Black wild cumin has a much different flavor than regular cumin. If you can't find it, substitute a teaspoon of regular (white) cumin.

- 2 pounds trimmed bitter melons
- 3 teaspoons salt
- ¼ cup oil
- 1 tablespoon black wild cumin seeds
- 1 teaspoon turmeric
- 1 tablespoon finely chopped ginger
- 2 green chile peppers, very finely chopped
- 3 large onions, chopped medium-fine
- 1 teaspoon mango powder
- ½ cup water

Wash the bitter melons and trim the tips. Cut them through lengthwise, then scrape out the white (sometimes pinkish-red on larger melons) cavity pulp and seeds. Cut the prepared melons crosswise into ½-inch strips. Place them in a dry bowl and toss with salt. Leave to stand for about 1½ hours.

Rinse away the salt with several changes of water, then let them stand in fresh water while you chop the onion.

Drain the melons and pat dry with a paper towel. Heat oil in a skillet and add the melon, stirring until they are cooked but not burnt. This takes about 20 minutes. Add the wild cumin, turmeric, ginger, and chopped pepper. Stir quickly and add the sliced onion.

Stir-fry until the onion is fully cooked and golden. Stir in the mango powder, then add water, and cover. Reduce the heat to low and cook for 5 more minutes. Serve hot with roti or chapatis.

Breakfast Raita

Type: Indian
Speed: Very fast
Notes: For many years this was almost a ritual after running on the beach with my friend and her dog first thing in the morning. Along with some roti and pickle, this is my absolute favorite way to start the day. Some testing of yogurts may be necessary to find one that is not sweet and can be warmed without breaking down. Nonvegan vegetarians can use regular plain unsweetened yogurt. I have tested many nondairy brands, and I think it is easiest to tell you what you don't want to use. Avoid sweetened or sweet-tasting yogurt and all the better if you can find something that has a slight sour taste. Soy and coconut yogurt seem to work best, but as brands can be quite regional you will have to experiment.

Starters & Side Dishes

- 2 tablespoons oil
- 1 tablespoon panch phoron spice mix*
- ¼ teaspoon asafetida
- 5 curry leaves
- 2 small green chiles, stemmed, seeded, and finely chopped
- 1 tablespoon finely chopped fresh ginger
- 2 tablespoons frozen small peas, defrosted
- ½ cup nondairy unsweetened yogurt

*Equal parts cumin seeds, yellow mustard, fennel, fenugreek, and nigella seeds

Make sure all the ingredients are ready by the stove. Heat the oil in a large skillet. Add the panch phoron. Once the mustard seeds in the mix start cracking, reduce the heat to medium-low. Add the asafetida, immediately followed by the curry leaves and a moment later the chile and ginger. Stir until the chile and ginger are cooked through, about a couple minutes. Add the peas and cook for 2 more minutes. Turn the heat off and stir in the yogurt. If the skillet is hot enough to warm the yogurt you can move it into a shallow dish. If not, carefully warm it on low heat, but do not bring to a boil or it will separate. Move it into the dish as soon as it is warm before the edge of the yogurt is bubbling. Serve this with Roti (page 33), Lime Pickle (page 158), and a little leftover Indian side dish like Dal (page 235) or Bitter Melon with Onion (page 60).

Brussels Sprouts in Rutabaga Sauce

Type: Indian
Preparation: You will need Rutabaga Base Sauce (page 24)
Speed: Very fast

- ½ cup water
- ¼ teaspoon salt
- 1 cup Rutabaga Base Sauce (page 24)
- ½ pound small brussels sprouts, trimmed

Bring the water and salt to a boil. Add the brussels sprouts, reduce the heat, and simmer for about 10 minutes. The sprouts should still be hard. Add the sauce, bring to a boil, reduce the heat, cover, and simmer for 5 minutes. Stir occasionally and add a little water if the pan is drying out.

Serve hot.

Cabbage Curry

Type: Indian
Preparation: You will need North Indian Base Sauce (page 22)
Speed: About 30 minutes
Notes: I have made the amounts to accommodate a whole cabbage. You can bring it to a more reasonable size by using half a cabbage and halving the amounts of the other ingredients. This is a great side dish to accompany Samosas (page 39) or eat with Chapatis (page 32).

- ¼ cup oil
- 1½ teaspoons black mustard seeds
- 1 tablespoon coconut oil
- 1 teaspoon cumin seeds
- 1 tablespoon finely chopped ginger
- 3 cloves garlic, finely chopped
- 1 large onion, chopped
- 1 tablespoon roasted coriander seeds, ground
- 1 teaspoon cayenne pepper
- 1 teaspoon turmeric
- 1 teaspoon salt
- 2 cups North Indian Base Sauce (page 22)
- 1 cup water
- 1 medium cabbage (about 2 pounds trimmed and chopped)
- 1 teaspoon garam masala
- 1 tablespoon mango powder
- 1 teaspoon besan (chickpea flour)

Heat oil in a large skillet. Add the mustard seeds. Once they start cracking, add the coconut oil. As soon as it melts, add the cumin seeds. Stir for a minute, then add the ginger, garlic, and onion. Fry the onion until it is golden. Add the coriander, cayenne, turmeric, and salt. Stir and then add the base sauce, water, and cabbage. Stir to make sure the cabbage is coated, then transfer to a large saucepan. Bring to a boil, then reduce the heat and simmer partly covered for 20 minutes. After 10 minutes, remove the lid to thicken the sauce. The cabbage should be fully cooked. Mix the garam masala, mango powder, and besan in a small bowl so there are no lumps. Stir into the cabbage and serve hot.

Cabbage Tagine

Type: North African
Speed: About an hour
Notes: Here's a simple cabbage side dish easily prepared and cooked in a tagine (page 8).

(page 8)

- ¼ cup olive oil
- 1 head of tight green cabbage (about 2 pounds), cut into 8 segments
- 1 onion, peeled and quartered
- 1 Preserved Lemon (page 165), coarsely chopped
- 1 large tomato, coarsely chopped
- 1½ teaspoons caraway seeds, ground
- 1 teaspoon dill seeds, crushed
- ½ teaspoon salt
- 2 tablespoon golden raisins
- 1 tablespoon chopped fresh parsley
- ¼ teaspoon cayenne pepper
- 1 tablespoon pine nuts
- 2 bay leaves
- 2 sprigs of fennel

Starters & Side Dishes

Prepare your majmar (page 8) or charcoal grill—outside only, of course. Pour the oil into the tray of your seasoned tagine and place the cabbage in, leaving a nest in the middle. Place the next 3 ingredients into the nest followed by the remaining ingredients over the top. Make sure the flames have died down from the charcoal and you have an even glow before placing the tagine on the majmar. If you are using a barbecue grill, you can roast vegetables at the same time as heating the tagine, but the pot must be at least 6 inches from the coals. Cook the cabbage until it is tender and the flavors have mixed. The exact time will vary depending on how hot the tagine is, and its size and thickness. In about 45 minutes the dish should be ready. You can serve it directly from the tagine (remember to use a heat-resistant mat), or turn it onto a serving dish.

Curried Watermelon

Type: Indian
Speed: About 30 minutes
Notes: This is quite spicy but light. Reserve the watermelon rind for Bharta (page 237)

- 1 cup watermelon juice
- 1 teaspoon cayenne pepper
- 3 cloves garlic, minced
- 1 teaspoon salt
- ¼ teaspoon turmeric
- 3 tablespoons oil
- ½ teaspoon carom seeds
- ½ teaspoon wild black cumin seeds
- ½ teaspoon black mustard seed
- 6 curry leaves
- ½ teaspoon ground coriander
- ½ teaspoon asafetida
- 1 teaspoon mango powder
- ½ teaspoon garam masala
- 3 cups watermelon cut into ½-inch cubes

Mix the first 5 ingredients together and set aside. Heat the oil in a skillet. Add the carom, cumin, and mustard seeds. When they start popping stir in the curry leaves, coriander, and asafetida. Once the leaves stop crackling, pour in the juice-spice mixture and bring to a boil uncovered. Continue to boil until the mixture is reduced to about half, then add the mango powder and garam masala. Stir and continue to boil to reduce to a medium thick sauce. Add the watermelon cubes and stir to coat with the sauce and heat through. Serve with rice.

Starters & Side Dishes

Fenugreek Purée

Type: Indian
Preparation: You can prepare the fenugreek (methi) ahead of time
Speed: About an hour plus trimming time
Notes: Considering the size of the fenugreek bundles this dish reduces dramatically, but it is so fragrant that just a couple of tablespoons per person is enough to add a big flavor to a meal.

Starters
& Side
Dishes

- 1 cup water
- ¼ cup whole green moong dal
- ½ teaspoon turmeric powder
- 1 green chile, minced
- 1 pound trimmed and washed fresh fenugreek leaves (about 2 pounds to start)
- 1 pound spinach, washed and trimmed
- 1 tablespoon minced ginger

- 1½ teaspoons salt
- 1 tablespoon coconut oil
- 1 tablespoon oil
- 1 medium onion, finely chopped
- 2 cloves garlic, chopped
- ½ teaspoon cayenne pepper
- ½ teaspoon mango powder
- 4 peppercorns, ground
- ½ teaspoon brown sugar
- 1 teaspoon garam masala

In a large saucepan, bring the water to a boil. Add the moong, turmeric, chile, fenugreek, spinach, and ginger. Once the fenugreek and spinach wilt, stir down and cover on a very low simmer. Make sure the pan doesn't dry out. If it gets too dry, add a little water. After about half an hour, let cool and move the mixture into a food processor with the salt. Blend into a paste.

   In a large skillet, heat the oils and fry the onion and garlic until golden brown. Stir in the cayenne and mango powder followed by the fenugreek-spinach paste, pepper, and sugar. Stir in half the garam masala, heat through, and serve with the second half of the garam masala sprinkled on top as a garnish.

Flavored Moong Dals

Type: Indian
Preparation: You will need a portion (about 4 cups) of Moong Dal Base (page 21) for each of the following recipes
Speed: Very fast
Notes: These are a few flavoring ideas for a moong dal to accompany an Indian meal.

Moong Dal with Cumin

- 1 tablespoon vegetable oil
- 1 teaspoon cumin seeds
- 1 portion Moong Dal Base
- A few cilantro leaves, chopped

Starters & Side Dishes

Heat the oil in small frying pan until almost smoking, then remove from the heat. Toss in cumin seeds and stir quickly for a few seconds. Be very careful not to burn, but it should turn a shade lighter. Pour immediately onto cooked dal, mix in, and serve. Garnish with a few chopped cilantro leaves.

Moong Dal with Ginger and Chile

- 3 tablespoons vegetable oil
- 1 teaspoon cumin seeds
- 1 tablespoon finely chopped fresh ginger
- 3 small green chiles, finely chopped
- 1 portion Moong Dal Base
- 1 tablespoon lemon juice
- ⅛ teaspoon cayenne pepper
- 2 tablespoons cilantro leaves, chopped, reserve a little for garnish

Heat the oil in small frying pan. Add cumin seeds and let sizzle for a few seconds. Add the ginger and chiles and fry for a minute before mixing into cooked dal along with lemon juice, cayenne, and cilantro. Serve garnished with more chopped cilantro.

Moong Dal with Garlic

- 6 tablespoons vegetable oil
- 6 large garlic cloves, finely sliced
- 1 portion Moong Dal Base

Fry garlic until golden brown, then mix into cooked dal.

Moong Dal with Black Mustard Seeds

- 2 tablespoons vegetable oil
- 1 teaspoon black mustard seeds
- 2 small green chiles, finely chopped
- 1 portion Moong Dal Base
- Chopped cilantro leaves for garnish

Heat the oil in a small frying pan until quite hot. Add the mustard seeds and fry until they splatter. Keep the lid handy to stop the seeds from flying all over the kitchen. Add the chiles and stir for a minute before mixing into cooked dal. Garnish with cilantro leaves.

Moong Dal with Onion and Tomato

- 1 portion Moong Dal Base
- ½ teaspoon minced ginger
- 1 clove garlic, minced
- 2 small green chiles, finely chopped
- 2 tablespoons vegetable oil
- ¼ teaspoon black mustard seeds
- 1 small onion, chopped
- ¼ teaspoon black onion seeds (nigella)
- 3 dry red chiles
- 1 ripe tomato, diced
- Chopped cilantro leaves for garnish

Starters & Side Dishes

Add the ginger, garlic, and chiles into the dal and bring to a boil. Simmer for 5 minutes, adding a little water if the dal becomes too thick. In a small frying pan, heat the oil and add the black mustard seeds. Once they start popping, add the onion and fry until it's golden brown. Then add the black onion seeds and chiles. Add chopped tomato and fry until the tomato is cooked and the oil starts to separate. Mix into dal, then garnish with cilantro leaves.

Moong Dal with Mango

- 5 tablespoons vegetable oil
- 1 teaspoon cumin seeds
- 1 green mango, peeled, pitted, and sliced
- ½ teaspoon cayenne pepper
- 1 teaspoon garam masala 1 portion Moong Dal Base
- 4 tablespoons cilantro, chopped, reserve some for garnish

Heat oil in small frying pan. Add cumin seeds and let sizzle for a few seconds, then add mango slices and fry for about 10 minutes on medium heat. Sprinkle on cayenne and garam masala, stir for a few seconds, and mix into cooked dal. Mix in most of the cilantro and serve garnished with the rest.

Moong Dal with Tomato and Spices

- 1 portion of Moong Dal Base
- 5 small green chiles, trimmed, seeded, and split lengthwise
- 7 tablespoons vegetable oil
- 1 large onion, minced
- 1 tablespoon minced ginger
- 1 large ripe tomato, finely chopped
- 1 tablespoon panch phoron spice mix*
- 6 curry leaves
- 4 dry red chiles
- 1 tablespoon minced garlic

*Equal parts cumin seeds, yellow mustard, fennel, fenugreek, and nigella seeds

Add the chiles to the dal and bring to a boil and simmer for 10 minutes. Add a little water if the dal becomes too thick. Heat 5 tablespoons oil in large frying pan and fry onion until golden. Add the ginger and tomato. Fry while stirring until the contents are cooked, about 10 minutes, and then mix into cooked dal. Heat the remaining 2 tablespoons of oil in a small saucepan. Add the panch phoron and let sizzle until the seeds pop. Add curry leaves for only a few seconds, then add the garlic. Keep stirring for half a minute, fold into the dal, and serve.

Green Beans in Tomato Sauce

Type: Turkish/Arabian
Speed: Less than an hour
Notes: I think I first ate this dish in Turkey, but variations can be found in many other countries in the region. The oil and tomatoes form a delicious sauce, which is perfect to eat with pita bread. Choose tender green beans that are not stringy. I like runner beans the best, but sometimes you have to trim away any string along the edge. You can also make this dish North African–style using a tagine (page 8). Pour the oil in first. There is no need to sauté the onions; simply arrange ingredients in the tray and cook it over a glowing majmar or barbecue.

- 1 large onion, chopped
- ¼ cup olive oil
- 2 cloves garlic, finely chopped
- ½ teaspoon caraway seeds, ground
- 1 pound flat green beans
- ¾ cup tomatoes, finely chopped
- 1 teaspoon salt
- 5 tablespoons tomato paste
- ½ cup water
- 1 tablespoon pine nuts

Sauté the onions for a few minutes, then add the garlic and fry until the onions are golden brown. Stir in the caraway and fry for a minute. Wash the green beans, trim the ends (removing any tough string), and cut into 2-inch pieces. Add the beans to the pan and fry for another 5 minutes. Now add the tomato, salt, tomato paste, and water. Stir, bring to a boil, then cover and reduce to simmer on low heat for half an hour. Stir occasionally, then mix in the pine nuts at the end of cooking. This dish can be served hot or cold and works well as a side dish.

Hummus

Type: Lebanese
Speed: Fast
Notes: Hummus is often the go-to option for a light vegan lunch, but supermarket hummus is usually dreadful. The garnish is crucial! I really don't like the addition of cumin to hummus (although I list it as a variation as some do like it) and generally prefer the classic version.

Starters & Side Dishes

- 2 lemons, juiced
- ½ cup tahini
- 3 medium cloves garlic
- ½ tablespoon salt
- ¼ small Preserved Lemon (page 165) (optional)

- 15-ounce can of chickpeas (wait before draining off the liquid) or 1½ cups cooked chickpeas
- Olive oil, paprika, and parsley for garnish

Place the lemon juice, tahini, garlic, salt, and preserved lemon in a food processor with 3 tablespoons of the liquid from the chickpea can (4 if you plan to eat the hummus the next day). Blend until smooth and no garlic chunks remain. Drain the rest of the liquid from the chickpeas (it can be discarded or saved for vegetable stock). Set 9 chickpeas aside and add the rest to the food processor. Blend until you get the desired consistency. I prefer a very smooth hummus, while others prefer more texture. Scrape down the sides of the processor and re-blend to ensure a lump-free paste. When you are happy with the consistency, taste for saltiness. Remember, various brands of chickpeas will differ in the salt content, so add more to taste and process in.

Put the hummus into a decorative shallow bowl and shake roughly flat. The paste should be light and somewhat movable. Pour a little olive oil (about a tablespoon) in the middle and work outward with the back of a spoon, sealing and flattening with oil (adding more oil if necessary). The result should be a flat, sealed surface with no puddles of oil. Using a single-holed saltshaker filled with paprika, draw a diagonal grid of 3 lines by 3 lines. (Make sure the paprika has no lumps and flows freely; you might want to test it on a piece of paper first). Moisten the chickpeas with a drop of oil and place each where the lines intersect (there should be 9 cross points.) Finally, garnish the perimeter with finely chopped parsley.

Tip: To mellow the garlic, slice and blanch in boiling water for a few seconds, or use grilled garlic.

Options

A: To make hummus with dried chickpeas, soak them overnight in plenty of water; they will almost triple in size. Drain and rinse. Discard any discolored chickpeas or floaters. Using fresh water, cover the chickpeas in a large pan and bring to a boil. Reduce the heat, cover, and simmer for 1½ hours. You will notice that I have omitted any portion amounts. I'm of the opinion that unless you are making a large batch of hummus for a party, or preparing to make multiple chickpea dishes. It's really not worth the energy to make one batch using dried chickpeas, as the canned variety is inexpensive. For larger batches you will need about ⅓ cup of dried chickpeas per portion. Remember to adjust the salt.

B: There are many hummus variations. Some additions are roasted red pepper, mint leaves, cumin, and olives. After mastering the basic recipe you can experiment with these ideas or your own.

C: The above recipe is presented in a formal manner. You can use this format to be creative with the garnish. You can substitute halved black olives or pine nuts in place of the whole chickpeas, or invent new patterns. Another option is to present the hummus in a less formal way. Normally this means a well in the middle of a portion of hummus filled with olive oil and sprinkled with paprika or za'atar. Hummus is often served with black olives or radishes and fresh pita bread. Restaurants in Lebanon are often very creative with their hummus art.

Starters & Side Dishes

Mango and Pineapple Curry

Type: Indian
Speed: Less than an hour
Notes: This savory starter can be served in the shell of the pineapple or in half pineapple skin boats. Alternatively you can use the shell for rice to tie in the theme.

- 1 medium pineapple
- 2 medium mangos
- 1 tablespoon coriander seeds
- 1 tablespoon finely chopped ginger
- 1 teaspoon cayenne pepper
- ½ teaspoon turmeric
- ¼ cup oil
- 1 teaspoon black mustard seeds
- ½ teaspoon cumin seeds

- ¼ teaspoon fennel seeds
- 1 onion, chopped
- 10 curry leaves
- ½ teaspoon salt
- ⅓ cup water
- 2 tablespoons oil
- ½ teaspoons asafetida
- 2 dry red chiles
- ½ teaspoon wild black cumin seeds

If you want to use the pineapple as a serving vessel, cut off the top and set it aside. Without breaking the skin of the fruit, cut around the inside with a sharp knife and remove the flesh with a spoon or melon scoop to about ½ inch from the base. Some juice will accumulate at the bottom; reserve 2 tablespoons in a small bowl. If you don't want to serve this inside the pineapple, simply trim the skin away and core the inside as you would to make rings. Remove the core and dice the flesh into ½-inch cubes and set aside in a bowl. You should have about a pound. Peel and chop the mangos similarly, discarding the stone, and put the pieces in the bowl with the pineapple.

Dry roast the coriander seeds and place them in a grinder. Grind to a powder. Place the coriander, ginger, reserved pineapple juice, cayenne, and turmeric in a food processor and blend to make a paste.

Heat the oil in a large skillet. Add the mustard seeds. Once they start to spit, add the cumin and fennel. Let sizzle for a few seconds, then add the onions and curry leaves. Fry for a few minutes until the onions are cooked but not burnt at the edges. Add the spice paste and salt. Swirl water into the processor and tip into the pan. Stir and fry for 2 minutes, then add the fruit. Bring the mixture to a boil, then cover and reduce to a simmer and cook for 10 minutes. Uncover and continue simmering until the sauce starts to thicken a little. This should take 5 to 8 minutes. Switch off the heat and let stand. Heat the 2 tablespoons of oil in a small pan and add the asafetida, quickly followed by the peppers and wild cumin. Let sizzle, then immediately pour over the curry fold a little and fill the pineapple or serve in a dish. Try to present the whole red peppers on top.

Muhammara

Type: Syrian/Lebanese
Preparation: You will need fire-roasted red bell pepper (page 16)
Speed: Very fast
Notes: This dip can be eaten like hummus with pita bread, but it is also an interesting addition for a falafel sandwich. You can even use muhammara as a pasta sauce. Pomegranate molasses can be found in many Middle Eastern markets or online.

- 1 pita bread (or about ⅔ cup breadcrumbs)
- ½ pound fire-roasted red bell peppers, chopped
- 2 cloves garlic, chopped
- 1 teaspoon ground roasted cumin
- ¼ Preserved Lemon (page 165) (or 2 tablespoons lemon juice)
- 1 tablespoon pomegranate molasses
- ½ teaspoon cayenne pepper
- ⅓ cup olive oil
- ½ cup walnut pieces

Break the pita into chunks and process it into breadcrumbs in a food processor. You should have about ⅔ cup of crumbs. Add the red pepper, garlic, cumin, lemon, molasses, cayenne, and olive oil. Blend until you have a smooth paste. Dry roast the walnut pieces in a frying pan for a minute, shaking constantly. Be careful not to burn them. Add to the processor and blend until the walnuts are assimilated but still have some texture.

Serve in a bowl garnished with a few walnut halves.

> **Option:** If you reserve a red segment of fire-roasted pepper, it can be sliced into an attractive garnish to lay around the muhammara or form a pattern on it, perhaps with pine nuts or whole walnuts.

Peanut Vada (Indian Fritters)

Type: South Indian
Preparation: 4-hour soaking time
Speed: ½ hour
Notes: This vada is particularly suited for a snack with some chutney. The trick with vada is to get the right relationship between the three variables: oil heat, frying time, and size of the vada. If the vada is too big, the interior will be raw unless you cook it longer and risk burning the outside. Too low of a heat and the vada will be oily. Too small and too hot and they will cook through like a cookie. So make the vada the size of a mini donut and fry in sizzling hot oil until they are golden brown. When the first one is done you might want to test it. The interior should have lost the raw taste and be cooked through yet remain soft.

- 1 cup toor dal
- ½ cup peanuts, dry roasted
- ¼ cup desiccated coconut
- 1 teaspoon salt
- 3 fresh green chiles
- 1 tablespoon finely chopped fresh ginger
- 1 teaspoon asafetida
- ½ teaspoon turmeric
- 1 tablespoon water
- 1 onion, finely chopped
- 2 tablespoons cilantro leaves, finely chopped
- 6 to 8 fresh curry leaves, chopped
- Oil for deep frying

Rinse and soak the dal for 4 hours, then drain. Lightly crush the peanuts in a mortar and pestle until they are in small chunks and set aside. In a frying pan, dry roast the coconut until there are no white pieces left and it is an even cinnamon color, then grind it in the mortar and pestle to a coarse powder.

Drain the dal and then blend it in a food processor along with the toasted coconut, salt, chiles, ginger, asafetida, turmeric, and water into a thick mudlike paste. Transfer into a bowl and mix in the peanuts, onion, cilantro, and curry leaves. Work with your hands until it will hold a shape.

Heat the oil in a deep frying pan (about 2 inches deep). With moist hands, form the paste into a flat patty about 2 inches across and ½ inch thick. Work your finger through the center and make a small donut shape. This can be tricky as the vada can break. If it does, re-form it and try again. Carefully lower the fritter into the hot oil and fry until it is a golden brown. As the first one is frying, make the next. When each one is golden brown remove them from the oil with a slotted spoon and place them on a paper towel–covered plate. You can keep them in a hot oven until they are ready to be served or you can eat them cold the next day.

Pine Nut Pâté

Type: Arabian
Speed: Very fast
Notes: This is a rich dip both in taste and in the pocket book. I like to serve it with pickles, pita bread, and salad. You could also serve it on crackers as an *hors d'oeuvres.*

- 1 cup pine nuts
- 2 cloves garlic
- ¼ teaspoon salt
- Juice from 2 lemons

- 1 tablespoon olive oil
- Pomegranate seeds, parsley, whole pine nuts, or mint for garnish.

Starters & Side Dishes

Blend all ingredients except the garnish in a food processor until smooth. Arrange on a plate and use your garnish of choice. I sometimes frame the paste with pomegranate seeds, which cuts the rich pâté.

Potatoes and Fenugreek

Type: North Indian
Speed: 30 minutes
Notes: Fenugreek (methi) was abundant in southern Europe before being cultivated in India but seems to have fallen out of favor. It has an aroma that can permeate the kitchen and indeed be tasted on one's skin the day after eating it. Fresh, it can be a bit difficult to find, but it is possible to fake this dish using dry methi. Still, it's certainly worth seeking out the fresh greens. Use only the leaves, discarding any flowers and stalks.

Starters & Side Dishes

- ¼ cup oil
- 1 tablespoon coconut oil
- 1 teaspoon cumin seeds
- 1 large onion, chopped
- 2 whole cloves
- 2 cloves garlic, chopped
- 1 tablespoon chopped fresh ginger
- 4 cups fresh fenugreek leaves (or 1 cup cooked fenugreek)
- ½ teaspoon cayenne pepper

- ¼ teaspoon ground black pepper
- ½ teaspoon turmeric
- 1½ teaspoon salt
- 1 teaspoon mango powder (or 2 teaspoons lemon juice)
- 3 large potatoes (about 2½ pounds), peeled and chopped into ¾-inch cubes
- ½ cup water
- 1 teaspoon garam masala

Heat the oils in a large saucepan. Add the cumin seeds. Once they start to sizzle, add the onion and cloves. After a couple of minutes, add the garlic and ginger and stir until the onion is golden brown. Mix in the fenugreek leaves and stir until they wilt. Add the cayenne, pepper, turmeric, salt, mango powder, and potatoes. Stir to coat the potatoes with the spices. Add the water and bring to a boil, then cover and simmer over low heat until the potatoes are cooked. After about 10 minutes put the lid slightly off to dry out the liquid. Mix in the garam masala and serve in a shallow bowl.

Red Radishes in Rutabaga Sauce

Type: Indian
Preparation: You will need Rutabaga Base Sauce (page 24)
Speed: Very fast

- ¼ cup water
- ¼ teaspoon salt
- 1 cup Rutabaga Base Sauce (page 24)

- ½ pound red radishes, trimmed and halved

Starters & Side Dishes

Bring the water to a boil with the salt. Add the radishes and simmer on low heat for 5 minutes. Mix in the rutabaga sauce and bring to a boil. Turn down the heat and simmer covered until the radishes become a little translucent in the center and are cooked through, about 10 minutes.

Serve hot.

Sambar

Type: South Indian
Speed: About 30 minutes
Notes: This dish is highly spiced and served as an accompaniment to almost every meal in the South. I have chosen to omit tomato, which some sambar recipes employ. I think it makes a nice change from the northern tomato-rich sauces and allows the tamarind flavor to show through.

- ½ cup toor dal
- 2 cups water
- ¼ teaspoon turmeric
- ¼ cup unsweetened desiccated coconut
- 1 tablespoon white poppy seeds
- 1 green chile, trimmed at the stalk end
- ¼ teaspoon tamarind concentrate, dissolved in 3 tablespoons hot water
- 12 curry leaves
- 1 teaspoon salt

- 1 cup whole small shallots, skinned and trimmed
- 1 tablespoon besan (chickpea flour)
- 3 tablespoons Sambar Powder (page 20)
- 2 cups water
- 2 tablespoons oil
- ½ teaspoon asafetida
- 1 teaspoon black mustard seeds
- ½ teaspoon cumin seeds
- ½ teaspoon fenugreek seeds
- 1 dry red chile

Rinse the dal in several changes of water until the water runs clear. Drain and then put the dal into a saucepan with 2 cups of fresh water and the turmeric. Bring to a boil, then reduce to a simmer and cover, leaving the lid slightly ajar.

Dry roast the coconut until it's light brown, adding the poppy seeds in the last few seconds, then grind to a powder. Place the powder in a bowl with the chile, tamarind water, curry leaves, shallots, salt, besan, and sambar powder.

When the dal is fully cooked (about 30 minutes) mash it until it is fairly smooth. Stir in 2 cups of water, then add the contents of the bowl. Bring to a boil while stirring, then reduce the heat to a simmer, again with the lid slightly ajar, for about 20 minutes on low heat.

Heat the oil in a small frying pan and add the asafetida, quickly followed by the black mustard seeds. As they start to pop, add the cumin, fenugreek, and dry chile, being careful not to burn the spices. Mix into the sambar and serve.

Savory Brussels Sprouts

Type: North Indian
Speed: About 30 minutes
Notes: This green-on-green side dish is especially attractive with yellow pulao rice.

- 2 tablespoons coconut, dry roasted
- 1 teaspoon coriander seeds
- 1 pound small brussels sprouts, trimmed and cleaned
- ¼ cup oil
- 1 teaspoon cumin seeds
- ½ teaspoon fenugreek seeds
- ½ teaspoon turmeric
- ¼ teaspoon asafetida
- 1 tablespoon finely chopped fresh ginger
- 1 green chile
- One bunch of fresh dill weed (about 1½ ounces), chopped without the thicker stems

Starters & Side Dishes

Dry roast the coconut and coriander seeds together until no white remains on the coconut and it is an even cinnamon color. Grind to a powder in a coffee grinder or mortar and pestle.

Bring a saucepan of salted water to a boil and add the brussels sprouts. Boil for 10 minutes, then drain in a colander. Meanwhile, heat the oil in a skillet. Once hot, add the cumin seeds. Stir, then add the fenugreek, turmeric, asafetida, ginger, and chile. Fry on low heat for a couple of minutes, then stir in the coconut-coriander mixture. Carry on frying and stirring until the powder is well mixed. Now add the drained brussels sprouts, turning them until they are well coated in the spice mixture and take on a glazed look. This will take a couple of minutes. Now add the dill and mix thoroughly. Cover and cook on very low heat for about 5 minutes. Check for saltiness; you may need ¼ teaspoon more. Serve hot.

Savory Indian Snack

Type: Indian
Preparation: 12 hours soaking. You will need an empty mustard bottle.
Speed: Less than an hour after soaking
Notes: This classic Indian-style snack mix is eaten as you would salted peanuts. In fact, adding a few roasted peanuts would also add some variety.

Starters & Side Dishes

For the dal:

- 1 cup whole green moong beans
- 4 cups boiling water
- ½ teaspoon garam masala
- 1 teaspoon mango powder
- 1 teaspoon salt
- ½ teaspoon chaat masala

Place the beans in a bowl and rinse them until the water runs clear. Drain them and return them to the empty bowl. Add the boiling water and let them soak until the next day.

Rinse the dal in a colander, pat dry with paper towels, and then arrange them in a single layer a baking tray to dry. Now mix the spices in a small bowl and prepare the shapes while the dal dries in a warm spot.

For the shapes:

- ¼ cup desiccated coconut
- 1 teaspoon coconut oil
- 1 cup besan (chickpea flour)
- ⅓ cup rice flour
- 1 teaspoon salt
- 1 teaspoon cayenne pepper
- ¼ teaspoon asafetida
- ⅛ teaspoon baking soda
- ½ cup water
- Oil for deep frying

In an iron skillet, dry roast the coconut until it is an even cinnamon color. Transfer it to a mortar and pestle and grind to a powder. Place it in a bowl and add the coconut oil while it is still warm. Sieve the besan. In the same skillet, lightly dry roast the besan until it turns a shade darker. Add it to the bowl along with the rice flour, salt, cayenne, asafetida, and baking soda. Thoroughly mix the ingredients, then add the water. Using your hands, work the contents into a thick mudlike paste.

Heat the oil about 2 or 3 inches deep in a skillet. Meanwhile, lay out a sheet of greaseproof paper on the counter. Fill a clean empty mustard bottle with the paste and put on the cap. Decide the width of the shapes you want to make and use scissors to trim away the tip of the cap to make the appropriate hole. Squeeze out some paste onto the paper, drawing a little donut, a spiral, sticks, a shape of your own liking, or a combination of shapes, 1 to 1 ½ inches each. Try to keep your designs small for this mix. Once the oil is hot, carefully drop your shapes in, but not more than a single layer at a time. After they turn a light chocolate brown, you can remove with a slotted spoon to a paper towel and continue with the next batch.

Once the shapes are finished, carefully drop the dal into the same oil. Move it around with a wooden spoon and fry until the beans are cooked. This does not take too long, perhaps only minutes. Turn off the heat and quickly drain the dal using a metal sieve and a Pyrex bowl. Shake as much oil from the dal as you can then drop them onto a paper towel to remove more oil. Place the dal into a bowl while it's still warm and add the spice mix. Toss until it is coated before adding your shapes. The savory spice snack is now ready to serve in small bowls.

Option: Place a papadom under the grill. Once it is cooked, take it out and immediately fold it like a taco shell, pulling the ends together to form a basket. Be quick, as you only have seconds before the papadom sets. Put a little mixture inside and repeat to make individual edible snack bowls.

Starters & Side Dishes

Savory Potato Cakes

Type: Indian
Speed: About an hour
Notes: Serve these cakes with a dal or soup to make a light lunch, or simply eat with some sweet chutney.

- 2 pounds potatoes, peeled and chopped
- 1 large cauliflower floret
- 1 carrot, trimmed and washed
- 1½ cups frozen peas, defrosted
- 2 tablespoons chopped fresh cilantro
- 1 teaspoon mango powder
- ½ teaspoon cayenne pepper
- 2 tablespoons water
- ½ teaspoon salt
- 2 tablespoons cornstarch
- 1 teaspoon cumin powder, dry roasted
- Oil for frying

For the batter:

- 1 tablespoon besan (chickpea flour)
- ½ cup all-purpose flour
- ⅛ teaspoon salt
- ⅛ teaspoon asafetida
- ¾ cup water

Boil the potatoes, cauliflower, and carrot in salt water until they are tender but not falling apart. Drain the pan. Remove the carrot and cauliflower, placing them in one bowl and the potato in another bowl. Add the peas, cilantro, mango powder, cayenne, water, and salt to the carrot and cauliflower, then mash to a paste.

Add the cornstarch and cumin to the potato, then mash coarsely. Let both bowls stand while you heat 1½ inches of oil in a deep frying pan or skillet.

Meanwhile, mix the batter ingredients in a blender and put into a bowl.

Dust your work surface with flour. Form the mashed potatoes into balls about the size of a golf ball. Flatten each into a round about the diameter of a coffee mug and about ½ inch thick. Make a depression in the middle with a spoon and ladle a walnut-sized spoonful of the vegetable mix into the center. Carefully fold up the edges to engulf the stuffing, sealing the potato over it. Pat back down to a hockey puck–shaped cake, then coat both sides with flour. Proceed until all of the potato and mixture is depleted. By this time the first ones you made will have hardened a little, making them easier to handle. The oil should be hot but not smoking. Dip the first cake into the batter and then carefully lower it into the hot oil. After a minute or so, carefully flip it over with a fork so both sides are golden brown. Transfer onto a paper towel–lined plate. Proceed until all of the cakes are finished. Arrange them on a platter around a bowl of dal or chutney.

Spaghetti Squash with Peanuts

Type: South Indian
Speed: About 30 minutes
Notes: I recommend cooking the squash for this dish in the microwave to reduce the chance of overcooking and destroying the strands. This dish goes well with Sambar (page 78) or Cashew Soup (page 47).

- 1 medium spaghetti squash (about 3 pounds)
- ¼ cup unsweetened desiccated coconut
- ¼ cup raw peanuts
- 3 tablespoons oil
- 1 tablespoon black mustard seeds
- 1 tablespoon urad dal
- 8 fresh curry leaves
- ¼ teaspoon asafetida
- 2 dry red chile peppers
- 1 tablespoon finely chopped fresh ginger
- 1 tablespoon finely chopped green chile
- 1 teaspoon salt

Starters & Side Dishes

Stab the skin of the squash with a knife, then cook it in the microwave on high for about 15 minutes. Let it stand for a few minutes, then cut it in half lengthwise (see tip below). Remove the seeds and center fiber. Tease out the strands onto paper towels, taking care to keep them as unbroken as possible. Lay out the "spaghetti" in a thin layer and pat it dry with another paper towel. Leave aside to dry.

Roast the coconut and peanuts in an iron skillet until the coconut turns a cinnamon color and the peanuts are very lightly charred. Remove the roasted ingredients from the skillet and add the oil. Once the oil is hot, add the black mustard seeds. As soon as the seeds start to pop, add the urad dal. After a few seconds, the dal will darken. Reduce the heat to medium-low and add the curry leaves, asafetida, and peppers. Stir quickly and add the ginger and chile. Fry for about 30 seconds stirring. Using your fingers, carefully add the spaghetti squash, pulling the strands apart that are clumped and folding it into the spice a bit at a time. Once it is all in and coated with the mixture, cook on low heat for a few minutes, aerating with a fork to prevent burning. Take care not to break up the squash strands. The result should be light, not stodgy. It is now ready to serve.

Tip: Using the microwave, the squash skin will be strong enough to use as a serving boat. Don't forget to save the seeds for roasting (page 234).

Spicy Long Beans

Type: Indian
Speed: About 30 minutes
Notes: This dry spiced green bean dish is a good accompaniment for a tomato rich gravy preparation such as Peas and Mushrooms in Gravy (page 116) or koftas (pages 85, 110, and 119) with Kofta Sauce (page 108). You can make it milder by halving or eliminating the chiles. If you can't find the Asian long beans, you can substitute a round bean variety such as Blue Lake Pole.

Starters & Side Dishes

- 1 large onion, finely chopped
- 2 cloves garlic, finely chopped
- 2 tablespoons finely chopped ginger
- 2 green chiles, trimmed and finely chopped
- 1 tablespoon oil
- 1 tablespoon carom seeds
- 1 pound long beans, cut into ¼ segments
- 1 teaspoon ground coriander
- ½ teaspoon salt
- ½ teaspoon Sambar Powder (page 20)
- 2 tablespoons water
- ¼ teaspoon garam masala

Heat the oil in a large saucepan over medium heat. Add the carom seeds and stir letting them sizzle for a second before adding the onion. Reduce the heat to low and continue to stirring until the onions turn a golden brown, about 5 minutes. Add the garlic, ginger, and chile and stir for another minute, then add the chopped beans, coriander, salt, sambar powder, and water. Cover the pan and reduce the heat to low. Simmer for 15 minutes or until the water has evaporated. Fold in the garam masala and serve hot.

Split Pea Koftas

Type: Indian
Preparation: Overnight soaking
Speed: Less than an hour
Notes: You can serve these patties with Kofta Sauce (page 108) or a little soup such as Apple Soup (page 45) with plain roti.

- 1 cup yellow split peas, washed and soaked overnight
- 1 teaspoon cayenne pepper
- 1 tablespoon finely chopped fresh ginger
- ¼ teaspoon asafetida
- 1 teaspoon ground coriander
- Juice from 1 small beet (about 2 tablespoons)
- I small onion, finely chopped
- 2 tablespoons besan (chickpea flour)
- 1 teaspoon salt
- Oil for deep frying

Starters & Side Dishes

Rinse the soaked split peas and put them into a blender along with the cayenne pepper, ginger, asafetida, coriander, and beet juice. Blend to a slightly textured paste, then move into a bowl. Add the onion, besan, and salt. Form into balls about 1 inch in diameter and deep fry until they are cooked through but not blackened on the outside. Lay them out on a paper towel ready for serving.

Stir-Fried Peppers and Mushrooms

Type: North Indian
Speed: Fast
Notes: The juice from the mushrooms will form a gravy, which goes well with rice or flatbread.

- 3 tablespoons oil
- 1 large onion, chopped
- 1 tablespoon chopped ginger
- 2 large cloves garlic, chopped
- 6 ounces baby red bell peppers or mild red chile peppers
- 1 pound small button mushrooms, cleaned and dried
- ½ teaspoon turmeric
- ½ teaspoon cayenne pepper
- 1 teaspoon salt
- 1 teaspoon ground coriander
- 1 tablespoon lemon juice
- 1 teaspoon cumin seeds
- 2 tablespoons desiccated coconut

Heat the oil in a skillet and fry the onion until it is golden brown. Add the ginger, garlic, and peppers. Continue to fry on medium heat until the peppers soften. Add the mushrooms and fry until they release their juice, then add the turmeric, cayenne, salt, coriander, and lemon juice. Dry roast the cumin and coconut until there are no white pieces left and it is an even cinnamon color. Reduce the heat to low and mix in the cumin and coconut.

Serve hot.

Stuffed Peppers

Type: Arabian
Preparation: 30 minutes soaking
Speed: About 1½ hours
Notes: The rice-stuffed pepper seems to be a mainstay for the vegetarian dinner party. It's usually unimpressive because the peppers are generally undercooked and the filling might as well be served separately, not to mention the often bland flavor. In the Middle East, once the peppers are stuffed, they are often cooked in a casserole dish. In this recipe I ensure that the peppers have a nice roasted taste before they are stuffed.

You can also bake the stuffed peppers in a tagine instead of the oven, but make sure the flames have died down or the bottoms of the peppers will burn.

Starters & Side Dishes

- ½ cup basmati rice
- ½ teaspoon salt
- 4 large yellow, orange, or red bell peppers
- 1 tablespoon olive oil
- 1 medium onion, finely chopped
- 2 tablespoons pine nuts

- 1 tablespoon golden raisins
- ¼ teaspoon ground allspice
- ¼ teaspoon sugar
- 1 tablespoon fresh dill, chopped
- 2 tablespoons mint leaves, chopped
- 2 tablespoons olive oil
- 2 medium tomatoes

Soak the rice with the salt in a cup of water for 30 minutes. Fire roast the peppers over a flame until blackened but not burnt through. Remove the skins, cut a hole around the stalks to carefully remove them, and set the peppers aside.

Bring the rice to a boil, then reduce and simmer for about 10 minutes until all of the water is absorbed. Set the rice aside to cool a little.

Heat the olive oil in a skillet and fry the onion for about 5 minutes. Add the pine nuts and raisins and fry for another 3 minutes, making sure not to burn the onions. Transfer the onion mixture to a mixing bowl and add the allspice and sugar. Add the cooked rice, half of the dill, mint, and additional oil.

Cut four "caps" by slicing two domes from each tomato, which will fit the open end of each pepper. Set aside. Finely chop the remaining tomato and fold into the rice. Return the mixture to a saucepan, add a little water (about 1 to 2 tablespoons), and simmer on low heat for about 10 minutes. Add a little water if it dries out.

Let the mixture cool a little, dry off the peppers with a paper towel, and stuff each one carefully so as not to rip the delicate flesh. Cap each with the reserved tomato domes to prevent the filling falling out.

Preheat the oven to 350°F.

Grease a casserole dish with olive oil and stand the peppers upright in it. Then grease the tomato caps with a little olive oil and sprinkle on some salt.

Bake the peppers for 35 to 40 minutes until the caps are cooked, then serve arranged on a plate garnished with the rest of the dill.

Sweet Potatoes with Scallions

Type: Indian
Speed: About 30 minutes
Notes: This vegetable side dish makes a colorful addition to a southern Indian meal. In India, scallions are often fried as one would regular onions. Their taste is very distinctive. You can also substitute yams for a less-sweet version.

- 2 pounds sweet potatoes (or yams)
- 10 ounces scallions
- ¼ cup oil
- 1 teaspoon black mustard seeds
- 1 tablespoon dry urad dal
- ¼ teaspoon cayenne pepper
- 1 teaspoon turmeric
- ½ teaspoon ginger powder
- 1 teaspoon mango powder
- 1 tablespoon salt
- 1 cup water

Peel the sweet potatoes and slice them into ¼-inch rounds. Rinse and set aside. Trim the root end off the scallions, wash away any dirt, and chop into ¼-inch pieces.

Heat the oil in a deep, wide frying pan. Once it is almost smoking hot, add the mustard seeds. As soon as they start popping, add the urad dal. After a few seconds, being careful not to let the dal burn, add the cayenne, turmeric, ginger, mango, and salt. Add the scallions and stir the contents together. Now add the sweet potato and water. Bring to a boil, cover, and reduce to a simmer for 10 minutes. Remove the lid and let the excess moisture evaporate another 5 minutes. Serve in an open bowl to display the colors of the vegetables.

Thanks for Giving Me What I Didn't Want

From a decadent backstreet "Mafia"-type establishment on the Italian leg of the Ramones tour to an intimate bistro in Brazil, promoters would regularly try to score points by taking us for a lavish meal. They normally had an arrangement with a local restaurant to receive a reduced rate in return for a conduit to the celebrities passing through town. How better to impress than to serve the local delicacy, whatever that might be? Unfortunately, the more lavish the feast was for most, the worse it was for the vegan or vegetarian. This, for me, highlights the arrogance of the mainstream when it assumes the more death a meal involves the more impressive it is.

Main Courses

I have been either vegan or vegetarian for more than forty years. In that time I have come to believe that the premise of trying to emulate "mainstream" food is flawed. We shouldn't be chasing the textures and flavors of those cuisines but either creating new ones or, as I have mostly chosen to do in this book, looking at traditionally established vegan dishes.

For the vegetarian, dairy is available but still the temptation is to make veggie burgers or soy sausages. I too will eat a veggie burger from time to time—it's fast and easy and of course it's comfort food—but really what is a falafel but an ancient veggie burger? When it comes to a thanksgiving Tofurky of fake poultry, however, I'm no longer interested. At the risk of sounding naïve, I reject the premise of mimicking a meat-based diet because I reject the conventions of a society that supports it. Imitation is the sincerest form of flattery, and I have nothing flattering to say about the misery we visit on animals.

For the purpose of this book, the concept of a main course remains vague. The best I can say is that the dishes in this section will generally create a sufficiently substantial serving, together with a few accompaniments, to constitute a meal. However, these recipes, and those in the previous "Starters & Side Dishes" chapter, are interchangeable and somewhat arbitrary. Most of these dishes can be relegated to side dish for a larger group or served as an element in a buffet setting.

However you present the table, dishes like North African Flavored Pasta (page 142) or Fennel in Nut Sauce (page 102) would certainly fit the bill as a dramatic focus. A good starting point is to try to eliminate duplication unless it's for dramatic effect. So, except in the case of a large buffet, you wouldn't want to serve Moong Dal (page 67) and Fried Dal (page 103) or Cauliflower, Potato, and Methi (page 97) with Potatoes and Cauliflower in Gravy (page 118). Instead, try to balance sweet and sour, spicy and mild, wet and dry, greens with starch, etc. Drinks, desserts, pickles, and side dishes should all complement each other. Also don't forget the colors and textures. These too can be balanced or matched to enhance the eating experience. An example would be to surround Fūl Mudammas (page 104) with Cucumber Salad (page 139) and then garnish the Fūl with chives to match the green.

As I mentioned, you might duplicate for effect: Split Pea Koftas (page 85), Red Cabbage Koftas (page 119), and Lotus Root Koftas (page 110) could be arranged around a bowl of Tomato Chutney (page 168). Or you could present a mixture of Falafels (page 101) and Lima Bean Patties (page 109) around a bowl of Taratoor Sauce (page 146). This idea builds an interesting hub to design a meal around.

In the Recycled section

Bananas in Nut Sauce

Type: Indian
Preparation: You will need White Nut Sauce (page 25)
Speed: About 30 minutes
Notes: Fry the bananas as quickly as you can after slicing them so they don't go brown. You can reserve the skins for Banana Peel Relish (page 221) if you process them quickly.

- ¾ cup oil
- 1 pound peeled bananas, cut into 1-inch rounds
- 1 tablespoon finely chopped fresh ginger
- 1 green chile, chopped
- 1 medium onion, chopped
- 2 tablespoons fresh cilantro leaves, chopped
- ½ teaspoon fennel seeds
- 1 teaspoon black mustard seeds
- 1 teaspoon cumin seeds
- 1 stick cinnamon
- Seeds from 3 cardamom pods
- 4 whole cloves
- 6 fresh curry leaves
- 1 cup White Nut Sauce (page 25)
- 1 teaspoon salt
- 1 tablespoon lemon juice
- ½ cup water

Main Courses

Heat the oil in a skillet until it is quite hot, then add the bananas and fry until they are an even golden brown. Remove with a slotted spoon and set aside.

In a food processor, blend the ginger, chile, onion, and cilantro to a paste. Set aside. Reheat the remaining oil, then add the fennel, black mustard, and cumin. Once the mustard starts to pop, add the cinnamon, cardamom, cloves, and curry leaves. Watch out for splattering oil when the leaves go in. Stir-fry for a minute, then add the onion paste from the food processor. Fry on medium heat while stirring for 5 minutes, then add the nut sauce, salt, lemon juice, and water. Bring to a boil, then reduce the heat, add the fried bananas, and simmer for a minute. Serve in a decorative shallow bowl.

Baingan Bharta

Type: North Indian
Preparation: You will need fire-roasted eggplant (page 15)
Speed: Less than an hour
Notes: I'm convinced this North Indian classic is better the next day. The flavors seem to intensify overnight in the refrigerator. If you have no fire-roasted pulp prepared, you'll need to roast a couple of very large eggplants.

- ½ cup oil
- ½ teaspoon black mustard seeds
- ½ teaspoon cumin seeds
- 3 cloves garlic, finely chopped
- 2 tablespoons finely chopped fresh ginger
- 2 large onions, chopped
- 2 large tomatoes, finely chopped
- 2 ½ cups roasted eggplant pulp, drained (page 15)
- 1 tablespoon salt
- ½ teaspoon turmeric
- 2 green chile peppers, chopped
- ¾ cup frozen green peas, defrosted
- 3 tablespoons cilantro, finely chopped

Main Courses

Prepare the ingredients and have them next to the stove. Heat the oil in a large skillet. Once hot, add the mustard and cumin seeds. When the mustard starts popping, add the garlic and ginger, sizzle quickly and then add the onion. Sauté until the onion is golden brown, about 10 minutes. Now add the eggplant pulp. Keep stirring, as the eggplant has a tendency to easily burn and build up a crust. This should take another 10 minutes. Add the tomato, salt, turmeric, and chile. Keep folding the mixture over medium heat for about 10 minutes. By this time, the tomato pieces should collapse and the oil start to separate out. Add the peas and cook stirring for another 5 minutes until the peas are cooked through. Mix in the cilantro, reserving a tablespoon for garnish, and serve.

Bitter Melons with Coconut

Type: Indian
Preparation: 1½ hours soaking
Speed: About 30 minutes
Notes: Don't shoot the messenger. Bitter Melon is, well, bitter. Here it is checked by the use of salt to draw out the juice. The highly textured Indian melons are much stronger, so perhaps you can first acquire the taste with the milder and smoother Chinese variety.

- 1 pound bitter melons
- 1 tablespoon salt for soaking
- 2 tablespoons plus 3 tablespoons vegetable oil
- 1 large onion, chopped
- ¼ teaspoon ground black pepper
- ¼ teaspoon ground cinnamon

- ¼ teaspoon asafetida
- ¼ teaspoon chili powder
- ⅔ cup desiccated coconut
- 1 teaspoon black mustard seeds
- 2 tablespoons brown sugar
- 1 teaspoon salt

Main Courses

Wash the bitter melons and trim the tips. Halve them lengthwise, then scrape out the white seeds (sometimes pinkish-red on larger melons) along with the cavity pulp. Cut the prepared melons crosswise into ¼-inch strips. Place them in a dry bowl and toss with the salt and leave to stand for about 1½ hours.

Rinse away the salt with several changes of water, then let the melons stand in fresh water while you fry the onion.

In a large skillet, fry the onion in 2 tablespoons of oil to a light golden color, about 5 minutes. Stir in the pepper, cinnamon, asafetida, and chili powder. Once the spices are completely mixed in, add the coconut and continue stirring for another 3 minutes. Allow the mixture to cool a little, then tip it into a food processor. Process to a paste and set aside.

Drain the melons and pat dry with a paper towel. Heat the 3 tablespoons of oil in a skillet, then add the black mustard seeds. Once the seeds start popping, reduce the heat to medium-low and add the melon, stirring until they are cooked, about 10 minutes. Do not burn. Add the paste from the food processor followed by the brown sugar and salt. Continue cooking and stirring for a few minutes to heat the paste through but make sure the melon remains in distinct pieces.

Serve warm.

Cabbage and Peas with Ginger

Type: Indian
Speed: Less than an hour
Notes: This is a nice dish to turn samosas and roti into a meal.

- ¼ cup oil
- 1 tablespoon black mustard seeds
- 1 teaspoon cumin seeds
- 3 tablespoons minced ginger
- 3 cloves garlic, minced
- 1 onion, chopped
- 1 tablespoon ground coriander
- ½ teaspoon turmeric

- 1 teaspoon salt
- 2 tomatoes, finely chopped
- 1 green chile, minced
- 1 small-to-medium cabbage, chopped
- 1½ cups green peas
- 1½ teaspoon garam masala

Heat the oil in a large skillet, then add the black mustard and cumin seeds. When the mustard seeds start popping, add the ginger and garlic, stirring briefly, and then add the onion. Sauté on low heat until the onion is golden brown, about 10 minutes. Stir in the coriander, turmeric, and salt. Immediately add the tomato and chile and sauté until the tomato is blended into the sauce. That will take about 10 more minutes, stirring frequently. Add the cabbage, stirring until it turns limp, 5 to 8 minutes. Add the peas and continue stirring for another 10 minutes. Fold in the garam masala and serve hot.

Cauliflower, Potato, and Methi Curry

Type: North Indian
Preparation: You will need North Indian Base Sauce (page 22)
Speed: Less than an hour
Notes: You can substitute other vegetables like carrots, green beans, rutabaga, etc. to total 2 pounds. Serve with Indian bread and sweet chutney as a snack or with rice and dal as a full meal.

Main Courses

- 3 tablespoons coconut oil
- ¼ cup oil
- 1 tablespoon cumin seeds
- 1 small cinnamon stick
- 3 cardamom pods
- 5 whole cloves
- 2 large onion, chopped
- 3 small green chiles, chopped
- 6 cloves garlic, chopped
- 1 pound potatoes, peeled and cut into large cubes

- 3 cups North Indian Base Sauce (page 22)
- 1½ cups water
- 1½ cups (packed) fenugreek leaves (methi), finely chopped
- 1½ teaspoon salt
- 1 pound cauliflower florets
- 1 tablespoon roasted besan (chickpea flour)
- 1½ teaspoon garam masala

Heat the oils in a large skillet. Add the cumin seeds, cinnamon, cardamom, and cloves. As soon as the cumin turns a shade darker, add the onion, chiles, and garlic. Stir-fry on medium heat until the onions are golden brown, about 10 minutes. Add the potato and fry for 2 minutes, making sure they are coated with the oil. Mix in the base sauce, water, and fenugreek. Bring to a boil, then reduce to a simmer and cover for a further 5 minutes. Mix in the salt and cauliflower, making sure it is coated with the sauce. Keep covered and simmer until the vegetables are soft but not falling apart, 10 to 15 minutes. Mix together the besan and garam masala and fold in to thicken the sauce. Serve hot.

Chana Masala with Chiles

Type: Indian
Preparation: Soak the chickpeas overnight and then boil them, unless you are using canned
Speed: Less than an hour
Notes: This chana masala version has a thick gravy and whole chiles. It's good with some roti and sweet chutney.

Main
Courses

- 2 15-ounce cans of chickpeas or 30 ounces cooked chickpeas with cooking liquid
- ½ cup oil
- 2 large onions, finely chopped
- 2 tablespoons finely chopped fresh ginger
- 4 cloves garlic, finely chopped
- About 8 large mild green chiles
- 1 teaspoon ground cumin
- ½ teaspoon ground cardamom

- 1 teaspoon ground turmeric
- 1 tablespoon ground coriander
- 1 tablespoon mango powder
- 1 teaspoon cayenne pepper
- 4 medium tomatoes, peeled and chopped
- 1 tablespoon salt
- 1 tablespoon garam masala
- 1 small onion, finely sliced into rings

Drain the chickpeas and set aside, reserving the cooking liquid. Heat the oil in a large skillet. Add onion, ginger, and garlic and fry until the onion is golden brown, about 10 minutes. Add the chiles whole (but with the stalk end trimmed) and stir until the chiles collapse, about 5 more minutes. Add the cumin, cardamom, turmeric, coriander, mango powder, and cayenne. Mix thoroughly, then immediately add the tomatoes. Stir over medium heat until the tomatoes become pulpy, this takes about 5 minutes. Add a cup of the chickpea cooking water and the salt. Simmer covered for 5 more minutes. Add the chickpeas and simmer for another 5 minutes. Stir in the garam masala. Transfer into a serving bowl and garnish with finely cut raw onion rings.

Crookneck Squash with Yellow Split Peas

Type: Indian
Speed: Less than an hour
Notes: In this recipe, I like to cook the split peas so they don't form a mash but stay whole.

- 1 cup yellow split peas
- 3½ cups water
- 1 teaspoon salt
- 1 teaspoon turmeric
- 1 large tomato, chopped

- 2 tablespoons Sambar Powder (page 20)
- 3 tablespoons oil
- 1 large onion, chopped
- 1 cup crookneck squash, diced

Rinse the split peas until the water runs clear. In a large saucepan, bring the peas, water, salt, and turmeric to a boil, cover and reduce the heat to a simmer for about half an hour. Add the tomato and cook for another 5 minutes, making sure it doesn't burn. Stir in the sambar powder.

Heat the oil in a skillet and fry the onion for about 5 minutes until it is a light golden color. Add the squash and continue to fry on medium-low heat until the squash is tender but not falling apart. Fold the onion and squash mixture into the peas, cover, and heat on low heat until any remaining water has evaporated. You should be left with a slightly moist yellow dal. Serve hot with roti or basmati rice.

Eggplant and Chickpeas

Type: North African
Preparation: 30 minutes soaking
Speed: About an hour
Notes: This casserole can be eaten hot over couscous (page 127) but somehow I prefer it cold with some salad and bread to sop up the gravy.

- 1 large eggplant
- 1 tablespoon salt
- 5 tablespoons olive oil
- 1 tablespoon vegetable oil
- 1 large onion, chopped
- 1 cinnamon stick
- 3 cloves garlic, chopped
- ½ cup olive oil
- 2 tablespoons vegetable oil

- 15-ounce can of chickpeas
- 6 tablespoons tomato paste
- 1 teaspoon salt
- ½ cup water
- ¼ teaspoon ground allspice
- ¼ teaspoon ground coriander
- 1 cup chopped tomatoes
- ¼ cup mint, chopped

Cut the eggplant into ½-inch slices, then soak them in salt water for 30 minutes. They will float, so weigh them down with a plate or even a sieve with a plate on top. Meanwhile, in a large skillet, fry the onion and cinnamon stick in the oils until golden brown, then add the garlic. Remove the onion and garlic from the pan with a slotted spoon, draining as much oil as you can. Remove the eggplant from the water and pat dry with a paper towel. Add the extra oils to the pan and fry the eggplant slices until they cook through. The eggplant will quickly absorb the oil. Continue to fry the slices while turning them and some of the oil will be released. Remove and arrange the slices in a casserole dish, then preheat the oven to 365°F.

Put the chickpeas, cooking liquid, tomato paste, salt, and water into the skillet. Bring it to a boil, then stir in the allspice and coriander, followed by the tomatoes. Boil for 10 minutes to reduce a little, then add the fried onion (remove the cinnamon stick).

Pour the tomato mixture over the eggplant and distribute evenly. Bake in the oven for about 25 minutes, then allow to cool.

Turn onto a dish and garnish with mint.

Falafel

Type: Arabian
Preparation: Overnight soaking
Speed: Less than an hour
Notes: Falafel can add dimension to a salad or be a meal along with shredded vegetables inside a Pita Bread (page 35) with tahini dressing. I usually keep a jar of dehydrated falafel mix in case I need a quick fix for lunch, but making fresh falafel from scratch is markedly better. This will yield between 20 and 32 falafels, depending on the size, enough for 8 or so people as a main course.

- 2 cups dry peeled fava beans
- 2 medium red onions, chopped
- 3 cloves garlic, chopped
- ½ teaspoon ground cumin
- 1 teaspoon ground coriander
- ¼ teaspoon ground black pepper
- ¼ teaspoon cayenne pepper
- 1 teaspoon baking soda
- 1 tablespoon salt
- 2 tablespoons fresh parsley
- Oil for deep frying

Main
Courses

Rinse the fava beans and soak them overnight. Rinse again and drain. In a food processor, blend all the ingredients together (except the oil) to make a stiff paste. Scrape down the sides to make sure all of the ingredients are blended. Let the mixture stand in a bowl while you prepare a deep frying pan or wide saucepan with oil about 3 inches deep. Knead the paste a little with your hands and as the oil heats form small burgers about 1½ inches in diameter and ½ inch thick. Once the oil is hot, lower a batch of falafels in. Fry until they are golden brown, making sure both sides are equally done. Transfer them to a plate lined with a paper towel and repeat in batches until complete.

Fennel in Nut Sauce

Type: Indian
Preparation: You will need White Nut Sauce (page 25)
Speed: About an hour
Notes: This fennel dish is rich and creamy and a small amount is very filling. Serve with a light soup and Roti (page 33).

- ¼ cup oil
- 1 teaspoon black mustard seeds
- 1 teaspoon cumin seeds
- 1 teaspoon fennel seeds
- 1 tablespoon dry urad dal
- 5 whole dry red chile peppers
- ¼ teaspoon asafetida
- 6 curry leaves
- 1 medium onion, chopped
- 1 fresh green chile pepper, chopped
- 1 tablespoon finely chopped ginger
- 2 fennel bulbs, trimmed and quartered, reserving greens for garnish
- ½ teaspoon turmeric
- 1 cup water
- 1 teaspoon salt
- 1 cup White Nut Sauce (page 25)
- Juice from ½ a lemon

Heat the oil in a saucepan. Add the mustard seeds, cumin, fennel, and urad dal. Once the mustard seeds start to pop, add the dried peppers, asafetida, curry leaves, onion, fresh pepper, and ginger. Fry until the onions become golden. Add the fennel bulbs and turmeric. Mix in the spices until the fennel is coated, then add the water and salt. Bring to a boil, then cover and simmer for 35 minutes. Fold in the nut sauce and bring back to a boil. Stir in the lemon juice and simmer for another 5 minutes. Serve in a shallow dish and garnish with a few fennel greens.

Fried Dal

Type: Indian/Pakistani
Speed: Less than an hour
Notes: I spent an interesting 8 days in Karachi in 2004. Unlike in India, vegetarian food is not so readily available in Pakistan. I did manage to find this dal in a small restaurant and ate it almost every day with chapatis.

- ½ cup red lentils
- ½ cup moong dal
- 2 cups water
- 1 teaspoon turmeric
- 1 large onion
- 3 fresh green chiles, stems removed and split lengthwise
- 1 cup peeled, chopped tomatoes
- 1 tablespoon salt
- ¼ cup oil
- ½ teaspoon black mustard seeds
- ½ teaspoon cumin seeds
- ½ teaspoon fenugreek seeds
- ½ teaspoon asafetida
- 2 cloves garlic, sliced
- 10 curry leaves
- 3 dry red chiles
- 1 tablespoon fresh cilantro, chopped

Main Courses

Combine the lentils and dal into a large saucepan and wash until the water runs clear. Drain, then add the water and turmeric. Bring to a boil. Meanwhile, slice the onion and add it to the pan along with the chiles. Reduce to low and simmer until the dal falls apart, about 20 minutes. Toward the end, help the process along with a potato masher. Stir in the tomatoes and salt and bring to a boil again. Turn once more to low and cover. If the mixture thickens too much, thin out with a little water, but you want the tomato chunks to fall apart.

Heat the oil in a small frying pan. Add the mustard, cumin, and fenugreek seeds. Fry until the mustard starts to pop. Add the asafetida. As it sizzles, immediately add the chopped garlic, curry leaves, and chiles. Do not allow to burn. Fold the fried mixture into the saucepan. Serve garnished with the fresh cilantro.

Fūl Mudammas

Type: Egyptian
Preparation: Overnight soaking
Speed: More than 2 hours (mostly simmering time)
Notes: Fūl is a popular breakfast dish in Egypt. It is made from the smaller dried fava bean variety *hammām*. They do not need to be peeled like the larger fūl rūmī variety. In this version I use a prepeeled, dried bean. For variation I sometimes use scallions or wild onion tops in place of the onion. There's a good reason the Egyptians eat fūl every day!

If you can only find the larger fava beans, peel them by soaking them overnight and then boiling them for 15 minutes to loosen the skin. Make a small nick in the skin and pop out the bean.

Main Courses

- 2 cups dried, peeled fava beans
- 7 cups water
- ½ cup red lentils
- 1 tablespoon salt
- 1 medium onion, chopped (or ½ cup chopped scallions/wild onions)
- 1 large tomato, chopped
- 2 cloves garlic, finely chopped
- ¼ cup olive oil
- Juice from 1 lime or lemon
- A little diced cucumber
- Paprika (optional)

Rinse the fava beans until the water runs clear, then soak them overnight. If you are using unpeeled beans, depending on the size, you will need up to double the amount.

Drain and rinse the beans and bring them to a boil in the additional water. Meanwhile, rinse the lentils until the water runs clear. Drain and add them to the pot along with the salt, onion, tomato, and garlic, then reduce to low heat.

Cook for a couple of hours covered. This may seem like an awful lot of water, but fūl is a dish that stews for a long time and it should slowly thicken. Leftovers the next day are often too thick and need to be watered down again.

You will not need to mash this version, as it will form a smooth porridge with stirring.

Put the fūl into a serving bowl or individual bowls and garnish with olive oil, lime or lemon juice, and diced cucumber.

Add a dash of paprika for a colorful flair.

Instant Celery Root Sambar

Type: South Indian
Preparation: You will need Celery Root Base Sauce (see Rutabaga Base Sauce page 24)
Speed: Very quick
Notes: Okay, it's not really instant, but it is quick and easy.

- 3 cups Celery Root Base Sauce (page 24)
- 15-ounce can of chickpeas
- ½ pound cauliflower florets
- ½ pound potato, peeled and coarsely chopped
- Cilantro leaves for garnish

In a large saucepan, heat the base sauce (defrost if it is frozen). Add the chickpeas with the cooking liquid and bring the mixture to a boil. Add the potato and boil for a few minutes, then add the cauliflower. Simmer covered for about 10 minutes until the vegetables are cooked through but not falling apart. Serve in a shallow dish garnished with cilantro.

Main Courses

Jackfruit in Coconut-Cashew Sauce

Type: South Indian
Speed: About 30 minutes
Notes: This is a rich, creamy dish in which the jackfruit flavor remains dominant. It should be served in small portions with a vegetable side dish and Roti (page 33).

- ¼ cup cashews
- 1 cup coconut milk
- 1 teaspoon ground coriander
- ¼ teaspoon ground black pepper
- ¼ teaspoon ground nutmeg
- 1 green chile, seeded
- 1 teaspoon salt
- 1 tablespoon chopped ginger
- 5 cloves garlic
- ¼ teaspoon turmeric powder
- 3 tablespoons oil

- 1 teaspoon cumin seeds
- 1 teaspoon black mustard seeds
- 10 curry leaves
- 1 onion, diced
- ½ cup water
- 1 tablespoon fresh cilantro, chopped
- ½ pound jackfruit segments, cut into fingernail-sized chunks
- 2 tablespoons cashew pieces for garnish

Place the first 10 ingredients in a blender and blend to a smooth paste. Heat the oil in a skillet and then add the cumin and mustard seeds. When the mustard seeds start popping, add the curry leaves (let crackle) and immediately add the diced onion. Sauté the onions until they are golden and add the blended coconut-cashew sauce. Swirl the water in the blender to loosen the contents and then pour into the pot. Bring the pot to a boil, then reduce to a low simmer. Add the cilantro and jackfruit, and simmer, stirring and mixing until the jackfruit becomes soft, about 8 to 10 minutes. The oil will start to separate a bit and the dish will become slightly glazed. Serve hot with cashew garnish.

Main Courses

Kale and Moong Bean Stew

Type: Indian
Speed: About 2 hours
Notes: This dish is quite filling and can be eaten like a stew with chapati or with rice.

- ½ pound kale, cleaned and coarsely chopped
- ¾ cup whole moong beans
- 4 cups water
- ½ teaspoon turmeric
- 1 cinnamon stick
- 1 teaspoon salt
- 3 large cloves garlic
- 10 sprigs of fresh cilantro

- 2 tablespoons chopped fresh ginger
- 2 to 4 green chiles
- ¼ cup oil
- 1 tablespoon cumin seeds
- 1 teaspoon black mustard seeds
- ¼ teaspoon fenugreek seeds
- 1 large onion, chopped
- 14-ounce can of diced tomatoes
- 1 teaspoon garam masala

Rinse the moong beans until the water runs clear. Drain and place them in a large saucepan with the fresh water. Bring the pot to a boil, then reduce to a simmer and add the turmeric and cinnamon. Cook on low heat for an hour, covered. Remove the cinnamon stick, then add the kale and salt. Cook for another 20 minutes. Add some water if it looks too dry.

In a food processor, make a paste out of the garlic, cilantro, ginger, and chiles (2 to 4, depending on the variety and how hot you prefer the dish). Set aside.

Heat the oil in a skillet and add the cumin and mustard. As soon as the mustard starts to pop, add the fenugreek seeds, sizzle for a minute, then add the onion. Fry until the onion turns golden brown, then add the tomatoes and fry until they are cooked, about 10 minutes. Stir in the garlic-cilantro-ginger-chile paste and fry for 3 or 4 more minutes.

Add the contents of the skillet to the saucepan and stir in the garam masala. Add more water if it's becoming too dry. Simmer for a couple of minutes before serving.

Kofta Sauce

Type: Indian
Preparation: You will need North Indian Base Sauce (page 22) and a batch of koftas
Speed: About 30 minutes
Notes: This sauce can be used for Split Pea Koftas (page 85), Red Cabbage Koftas (page 119), or Lotus Root Koftas (page 110).

- 1 tablespoon oil
- 1 tablespoon coconut oil
- 1 medium onion, finely chopped
- 1 teaspoon cumin seeds
- 3 whole cloves
- 3 cardamom pods

- 1 small stick cinnamon
- 2 cups North Indian Base Sauce (page 22)
- 1 teaspoon garam masala
- 1 tablespoon fresh cilantro, chopped

Heat the oils in an iron skillet. Fry the onion and cumin seeds for a few minutes, then add the cloves, cardamom, and cinnamon. Stir until the onion is golden brown. Add the base sauce and simmer on low heat for 5 minutes. Stir in the garam masala. If you need to thin the sauce, add a little warm water. Now add the koftas, making sure they are fully coated. Simmer until the koftas are heated through. Serve in a shallow bowl with the koftas in a single layer. Garnish with chopped cilantro.

Main Courses

Lima Bean Patties

Type: North African
Preparation: Overnight soaking
Speed: About an hour and a half
Notes: Like falafel, these patties can be used in a salad, in pita bread, with dipping sauce or even like a burger with onion, tomato, and lettuce.

- 2 cups dried lima beans, soaked overnight
- ¼ teaspoon sugar
- 1 teaspoon active yeast
- 1 tablespoon warm water
- 1 teaspoon Harissa (page 155) or chili powder
- 1½ teaspoon salt

- 5 cloves garlic, chopped
- 1 large red onion, chopped
- 1 teaspoon caraway seeds
- 1 teaspoon cumin seeds
- 1 teaspoon coriander seeds
- 2 tablespoons parsley leaves, or mint leaves, chopped
- Oil for deep frying

Main
Courses

Proof the yeast with sugar in warm water. In a food processor, blend the beans, proofed yeast, harissa, salt, garlic, and onion.

Dry roast the caraway, cumin, and coriander seeds and grind them in a mortar and pestle. Add to the processor with the parsley (or mint) leaves. You may need to blend in batches, but either way transfer to a bowl when you have an even paste and stir to blend every batch. Let the mixture stand for 30 minutes. Take a golf ball–sized portion of the mixture and shape into a small patty, like a tiny burger. Too big and the center will not cook through, too small and they will be too brittle. Repeat until the mixture is depleted, laying the patties out on your work surface. Cover the patties with plastic wrap and let them stand for 20 minutes. Meanwhile, prepare a shallow saucepan with oil for deep frying. Heat the oil until very hot but not smoking. Carefully drop the patties in but do not overfill. The patties should immediately sizzle. Once the patties are golden brown, roll them over.

Stack them on a paper-lined plate. Serve warm with salad, a dipping sauce and Pita Bread (page 35).

Lotus Root Koftas

Type: Indian
Speed: Less than an hour
Notes: Select pure cream-colored roots with no dark patches. This will make about 15 koftas. Serve with Kofta Sauce (page 108).

- 2 pounds lotus root (you will need 20 ounces after grating)
- ¼ cup desiccated coconut
- 1 tablespoon coriander seeds
- ¼ cup besan (chickpea flour)
- 1 tablespoon turmeric
- 1 teaspoon mango powder
- ½ teaspoon baking powder
- 1 teaspoon salt
- ½ teaspoon asafetida
- ½ teaspoon cayenne pepper
- Oil for deep frying

Scrape away the skin of the lotus root and run under the tap to remove any pieces of skin. Check for black spoiled areas inside the "tubes." Grate the root into a bowl and set aside. Dry roast the coconut and coriander seeds in an iron skillet until the coconut is an even cinnamon color, then grind to a powder in a mortar and pestle or spice grinder. Dry roast the besan in the same skillet and transfer with the coconut-coriander mixture into a second bowl. Mix in the turmeric, mango powder, baking powder, salt, asafetida, and cayenne.

Wring out as much juice as you can from the lotus root using your hands. Now mix it into the spice mixture and let stand for a few minutes while you heat the oil.

You will need to persuade the lotus koftas to form into a ball in your hands because they can resist a little, but after a few seconds they should hold firm. Make walnut-sized koftas and slowly lower them into the oil. Once they start to fry, they will hold together. After they are fully fried and are an even brown on the outside, remove them with a slotted spoon onto a plate until you have prepared the Kofta Sauce (page 108).

Main
Courses

Mushrooms in Nut Sauce

Type: Indian
Preparation: You will need White Nut Sauce (page 25)
Speed: Less than an hour
Notes: Eat this rich dish with Chapatis (page 32) or Roti (page 33).

- ¼ cup oil
- 1 teaspoon black mustard seeds
- 1 teaspoon urad dal
- ¼ teaspoon asafetida
- 2 dry red chile peppers
- 6 curry leaves
- 1 large onion, chopped
- 1 tablespoon finely chopped ginger
- ½ teaspoon turmeric
- ½ teaspoon cayenne pepper
- 1 teaspoon salt

- Seeds from 6 cardamom pods, ground
- 1 pound small button mushrooms
- 2 tablespoons tomato paste
- 1 cup White Nut Sauce (page 25)
- ½ cup water
- 2 tablespoons oil
- ½ teaspoon cumin seeds
- ½ teaspoon fenugreek seeds
- 2 cloves garlic, sliced

Main
Courses

Heat the oil in a skillet. Add the mustard seeds and urad dal. Fry until the seeds start popping. Add the asafetida, red peppers, and curry leaves. Once they start to sizzle, add the onion and ginger and fry until the onions are golden. Stir in the turmeric, cayenne, cardamom, and salt followed by the mushrooms. Stir-fry until the mushrooms release their juice, about 10 minutes. Fold in the tomato paste and fry for another minute, then add the nut sauce and water. Turn heat to low and stew for about 10 minutes.

Heat the oil in a small frying pan and add the cumin and fenugreek. As the seeds start to sizzle, add the garlic. Fry until it starts to turn golden and pour the contents of the pan onto the mushrooms. Mix the oil in and serve hot.

Masala Dosa

Type: Indian
Preparation: Overnight soaking and 8 hours fermenting
Speed: About an hour after soaking and fermenting
Notes: In southern Indian restaurants the masala dosa can be quite the showpiece dish, reaching almost 2 feet in diameter and wafer-thin. The secret to a successful dosa is the griddle or frying pan. Using a modern frying pan is just about impossible. My cook top has a griddle attachment, which works very well. A heavy, seasoned iron frying pan will also work, but if you try to make a dosa without the appropriate equipment, you'll most likely be digging the batter off the pan with a knife.

For the dosa:

- ¾ cup urad dal
- 1 teaspoon fenugreek seeds
- ¾ cup warm water
- 2 cups rice flour
- 1 tablespoon salt
- ½ teaspoon baking soda
- 1½ cups water

Rinse the urad dal in many changes of water until the water runs clear, then place it in a bowl covered by a few inches with water overnight with the fenugreek.

Drain the dal and put it into a food processor with the warm water to make a batter. Scrape the sides and reprocess to make sure there are no whole pieces. Move the batter into a bowl and add the rice flour, salt, and baking soda and stir, adding enough water to adjust the thickness to a pancake batter consistency. Make sure the batter is completely mixed, then set the bowl aside covered with plastic wrap in a warm place. It should be kept as warm as a hot summer day. I warm up the oven a just a little, then put the bowl in there. It needs to ferment the whole day, a minimum of 8 hours, so you will need to briefly reheat the oven a few times, but be careful not to get above 100°F.

For the filling:

- 2 tablespoons chana dal, soaked in water for ½ hour
- 2 large potatoes, peeled and cut into ¾-inch chunks
- ½ cup frozen peas, defrosted
- 3 tablespoons oil
- 1 teaspoon black mustard seeds
- 1 teaspoon urad dal
- 3 green chiles, chopped
- ½ teaspoon turmeric
- 2 tablespoons finely chopped fresh ginger
- 2 large onions, peeled and coarsely chopped
- 10 fresh curry leaves
- 1 teaspoon salt
- Oil

Boil the potatoes in salt water on medium heat until cooked through but not falling apart, about 6 or 7 minutes. Add the defrosted peas and boil for 2 more minutes. Drain and reserve the cooking liquid.

Meanwhile, drain and dry the chana dal, then heat the oil in a shallow, wide saucepan. Add the black mustard seeds. As soon as they start popping add the chana dal and urad dal, stir for a couple of minutes as the chana turns a shade darker. Add the chiles, turmeric, and ginger. Let it sizzle for a minute, then add the onion. Cook for about 5 minutes, then add the curry leaves. After stirring them in, add a half cup of the cooking liquid from the potatoes and the salt. Cover and simmer for several minutes.

Wipe an iron frying pan or griddle with oil and heat over a medium heat. It's best to use a scant amount of oil.

Test the filling by checking if a chana pea is still hard. If so, the filling is not ready. Once the chana dal softens, carefully fold in the potatoes and peas.

If a drop of water dropped onto the griddle immediately sizzles, it is hot enough, but the oil should not be smoking. My advice is to start small with your first attempt at a dosa, so ladle about ¼ cup of batter into the center of the griddle, then work outward with the back of a spoon, creating a thin, smooth layer. You will know after about a minute if your pan or griddle is working. The dosa should glide about with just the touch of a fork. Flip the dosa with a spatula after a couple of minutes. It should be golden brown. You can move it aside if you are using a griddle and re-oil the surface, then move it back. In a pan, add a drop of oil around the edge and work it in a little. Keep the dosas stacked on a plate in a warm oven ready to fill and serve while you make more.

Put about 3 serving spoons of filling in the center of a dosa, then fold it over and move on to the next until they are all finished.

Main
Courses

North African Flavored Pasta

Type: North African
Preparation: Fire roast and skin 2 yellow or red bell peppers
Speed: Less than an hour
Notes: This spaghetti recipe has the spicy flavors of North Africa. If you are not comfortable with spicy food, you can halve the cayenne pepper.

- 1 teaspoon ground coriander
- ½ teaspoon ground caraway seeds
- ½ teaspoon garlic powder
- 1 teaspoon cayenne pepper
- 5 black peppercorns, ground
- 2 tablespoons olive oil
- 5 large cloves garlic, thinly sliced
- 3 tablespoons chopped parsley
- 2 cups fire-roasted yellow or red bell peppers, puréed
- ¼ Preserved Lemon (page 165), finely chopped
- ½ teaspoon salt
- 2 tablespoons capers
- 1 teaspoon dried oregano
- 2 fire-roasted chiles
- 1 medium tomato
- 5 black olives
- About a pound long spaghetti
- Dash of olive oil

Put the first 5 ingredients together in a container next to the stove. Heat the oil in a skillet, then add the garlic slices, stir-fry for a few seconds, and then add the parsley, peppers, and lemon. Cook for about 10 minutes. Add the ground spices, salt, capers, and oregano, and cook for another 2 minutes. Set the sauce aside.

While the sauce is cooking, bring the salt water to a boil and add the spaghetti. While it cooks, blacken the chiles over a flame and remove the skins. Heat the grill and cut the tomato into thick slices. Drizzle a little olive oil over them and grill them until they start to shrink down and sizzle. Chop the chiles coarsely. Pit and slice the black olives.

Once the pasta is cooked, drain and arrange it like a nest in a large shallow bowl. Add the sauce to the center and garnish with the chiles, olives, and tomatoes. Drizzle with olive oil and serve.

Main Courses

Okra Northern Indian Style

Type: North Indian
Speed: Less than an hour
Notes: Many people believe that they don't like okra. It's not surprising, because when it is not prepared properly it's really slimy. Okra is exceedingly popular in India and is served stuffed and fried or, as in this recipe from the North, fried with onions and spices. I like to fry the okra and remove it from the pan. This lends better control to the cooking process of this delicate vegetable.

- 1 pound smallish, tender okra
- ⅔ cup oil
- 3 large onions, finely chopped
- 3 cloves garlic, finely chopped
- 2 tablespoons finely chopped fresh ginger
- 1 tablespoon ground coriander
- 1 teaspoon ground cumin
- ½ teaspoon cayenne pepper
- 1 teaspoon turmeric
- 1 teaspoon ground fennel
- ¼ teaspoon ground black pepper
- 1 teaspoon mango powder
- 1 teaspoon salt
- 2 large tomatoes, finely chopped
- 1¼ cups water
- ½ teaspoon garam masala

Main Courses

Trim the okra by shaving the thick end to a cone and snipping off the tip at the thin end. Heat the oil and fry the okra in a wide skillet until they start to brown, about 4 minutes. Remove the okra with a slotted spoon and add the onion to the same oil. After stirring the onions, add the garlic and ginger, then fry for about 10 minutes until the onions are golden brown. Add the coriander, cumin, cayenne, turmeric, fennel, pepper, mango, and salt. Stir until the spices are fully mixed in. Add the tomatoes and water, cover, and simmer for 5 minutes. Add the okra back to the pan along with the garam masala. Keep covered on low heat for another 15 minutes until the okra is tender but not falling apart. Carefully mix occasionally to avoid burning. Serve in a decorative bowl.

Peas and Mushrooms in Gravy

Type: North Indian
Speed: Less than an hour
Notes: Serve with Basmati Northern Style (page 126).

- ½ cup oil
- 1 teaspoon cumin seeds
- 4 whole cloves
- 4 cardamom pods
- 5 cups onion, coarsely chopped
- 10 cloves garlic
- 4 tablespoons finely chopped ginger
- 1 teaspoon turmeric
- 1 teaspoon cayenne pepper
- 2 teaspoons salt
- 2½ cups tomatoes, chopped
- 1 pound small button mushrooms
- 2 cups water
- 1 pound frozen peas, defrosted
- 1 tablespoon garam masala

Heat the oil in a large skillet. Once hot, add the cumin, cloves, and cardamom pods, let them sizzle, then immediately add the onion, garlic, and ginger. Stir until the onion is golden brown, then add the turmeric, cayenne, salt, and tomatoes. Continue cooking until the tomatoes are cooked and the oil starts to separate. Fold in the mushrooms to coat them and cook for about 10 minutes. Move the mixture into a large saucepan, add the water and peas, mix together, and bring to a boil. Immediately reduce heat to low, cover, and simmer, stirring occasionally, until the mixture becomes a thick gravy. Mix in the garam masala and serve.

Persimmons and Chickpeas with Anise

Type: Indian
Speed: Less than an hour
Notes: Persimmons come in two varieties: the Fuyu, which you eat hard like an apple, and the Hachiya, which must ripen to a jelly-like texture before eating. In season, the Fuyu persimmon tree produces so much fruit that the owners don't know what to do with it. They make a great juice mixed half and half with orange, or you can try this sweet and spicy Indian adaptation.

- ¼ cup chopped fresh ginger
- 2 medium sized onions
- 6 hot chiles
- ½ cup vegetable oil
- 1 small stick cinnamon
- 1 tablespoon cumin seeds
- 1 teaspoon fennel seeds
- 1 teaspoon anise seeds
- 2 tablespoons ground coriander
- 1 tablespoon ground roasted coconut powder
- 1 pound Fuyu persimmons (after peeling)
- 2 cups cooked chickpeas
- 1 teaspoon salt
- 1 tablespoon lemon juice
- 1 teaspoon garam masala

Main
Courses

In a food processor, mince the ginger, onion, and chiles to a paste.

Heat the oil. Once hot add the cinnamon, cumin, fennel, and anise. After a few seconds sizzling, add the paste. Turn the heat to medium-low and fry the mixture while stirring for about 10 minutes. Dry roast the coriander and coconut until there is no white left and the coconut is an even cinnamon color.

Peel and cut the persimmons into thick wedges (6 to 8 per fruit), add to the mixture along with the coriander-coconut mixture, chickpeas, salt, and lemon juice. Fold until the persimmons and chickpeas are evenly coated. Cover and reduce the heat to low and cook for about 15 minutes, stirring occasionally. Mix in the garam masala and serve.

Potatoes and Cauliflower in Gravy

Type: North Indian
Preparation: You will need North Indian Base Sauce (page 22)
Speed: 30 minutes
Notes: This dish is normally made using quite large chunks of potato and cauliflower florets. You can add half a teaspoon of cayenne pepper along with the cardamom pods to spice it up a little if you wish.

Main Courses

- 2 tablespoons oil
- 2 tablespoons coconut oil
- 1 medium onion, sliced
- 1 teaspoon cumin seeds
- 3 bay leaves
- 3 whole cloves
- 1 small stick cinnamon
- 3 cardamom pods
- 1 pound cauliflower florets
- 1 pound potatoes, peeled and cut into large chunks
- 1 teaspoon salt
- 3 cups North Indian Base Sauce (page 22)
- 1 tablespoon garam masala
- 1 tablespoon fresh cilantro, chopped

Heat the oils in a large saucepan. Add the onion, cumin seeds, bay leaves, cloves, cinnamon, and cardamom pods. Fry until the onion turns golden. Add the vegetables, tossing them in the spices for 1 minute. Add the salt, then immediately add the base sauce and bring the pan to a boil. Cover and lower to simmer for 15 minutes. The vegetables should now be soft, but not breaking apart. Stir in the garam masala. Serve in a deep bowl, garnished with fresh cilantro.

Red Cabbage Koftas

Type: Indian
Speed: Less than an hour
Notes: One thing I like about this particular kofta, apart from the colorful purple flecks, is that it really retains its cabbage taste. The kofta itself is quite springy and robust and it makes a great centerpiece for a dinner party.

- 2½ cups grated red cabbage
- 1 teaspoon coriander seeds
- 3 tablespoons desiccated coconut
- ⅔ cup besan (chickpea flour)
- 1 teaspoon turmeric
- 1 teaspoon mango powder
- 1 teaspoon garam masala
- 1 teaspoon baking powder
- ½ teaspoon cayenne pepper
- 1 teaspoon salt
- 1 tablespoon minced ginger
- Oil for deep frying

Grate the red cabbage (about one small head) into a bowl and set aside. Dry roast the coriander and coconut in an iron skillet until the coconut is an even cinnamon color and no white remains, then grind to a powder in a spice grinder. In the same skillet, dry roast the besan until it turns just a little darker. Break up any lumps. Place in a second bowl together with the coconut-coriander mixture, then add the turmeric, mango powder, garam masala, baking powder, cayenne, salt, and ginger. Mix thoroughly. Squeeze out as much juice as you can from the cabbage, then mix it into the spice mixture until it is thoroughly coated.

Heat oil about 2 inches deep in a wide shallow saucepan.

Work the mixture with your hands to form balls about an inch in diameter. You should find the remaining moisture in the cabbage enough to bind the kofta. I do them one at a time and then place them carefully in the hot oil. Once they are a rich brown, lift each one out with a slotted spoon and stack on a plate. You can eat them with some chutney or Tamarind Dipping Sauce (page 168) or serve them in Kofta Sauce (page 108).

Main
Courses

119

Tomato-Stuffed Eggplants

Type: Turkish
Speed: About 2 hours (1 hour of stewing)
Notes: There are a few vegan dishes common in most Turkish regions, but be careful. Often you will be assured there is no meat in a dish, but it is made with meat stock. This dish can also be served surrounded by couscous (page 127).

- 3 medium to large eggplants
- 2 tablespoons olive oil
- 2 medium onions, chopped
- ¼ cup olive oil
- 2 cloves garlic, minced
- 2 large tomatoes, chopped
- ⅓ bunch parsley, finely chopped
- 1 teaspoon plus ½ teaspoon salt
- ¾ cup water

Trim the ends of the eggplant. In a deep, wide frying pan, fry the eggplants in a single layer in the 2 tablespoons of oil until they collapse and are browned. Arrange them in pan so they do not move and slit them open lengthwise, stopping about an inch from each end. Keep the slits upward. Fry the onions in a separate frying pan in the ¼ cup of olive oil until golden brown. Add the garlic, fry for a few seconds, then add the tomatoes, parsley, and teaspoon of salt. Continue to fry for a quarter of an hour, until the mixture reduces to a sauce. Stuff the tomato mixture into the slits in the eggplants, then carefully pour the water around the eggplants and sprinkle the ½ teaspoon of salt over the top. Cover and simmer on low heat for about an hour, making sure the pan doesn't dry out. Turn off the heat and let the eggplants cool. There should be liquid left in the pan. Serve at room temperature in a shallow bowl with juice spooned around them.

Against the Grain

I grew up in a rural area of Leicester enjoying idyllic summers in the fields with my friends. Two local farm boys, the same ages as my elder brother and me, provided a veritable amusement park for us.. Between the spinney, our old Austin van (painted vaguely like the Batmobile and missing its doors), and various hay lofts, there was rarely a dull moment. We drove the old van around a field, which still had the remains of the ridge and furrow medieval strip farming. (Our half-acre garden also preserved this feature. Having been leased by the peasants from the King's holdings it was, and is still, called Kingsfield Road.) A game arose where half the kids would ride the van around, holding on for dear life as they were tossed about over the ancient furrows, while the others tried to capture the vehicle by physically ejecting the occupants out the back or side door holes. We ran our van on the endless supply of tractor fuel but had one small bottle of petrol, which was poured directly into the carburetor to start it. This pursuit was best enjoyed at night by flashlight.

During harvesting, all hands were on deck to bring in the straw and hay. The silos were full of barley and my team off-loaded the straw bales from the flat trailer into a cavernous barn. Strangely devoid of supervision, a tradition developed of building intricate three-dimensional mazes as each layer built. Once the barn was full, after a couple of days, a hideout was fashioned 30 feet up in the eaves of the barn, accessible only to the maze builders.

As the year unfolded, straw and hay would be consumed by the livestock leaving a substantial space in the middle of the barn. Here we would hang a rope swing from the rafters and alarmingly launch from the highest point of the remaining bales, landing safely in a deep pile of straw at the other side of the barn.

Barley was everywhere on the farm, but I don't ever recall eating it! I think it was bagged and shipped for animal feed. Nor did we seem to eat any grains directly as children, unless it was processed into bread or porridge oats. As I became old enough to travel into the city, Leicester's vast Indian community provided an opportunity to try various rice preparations for the first time. Rice was just about unheard-of growing up in the countryside, except perhaps for rice pudding.

Grains

Some rice dishes are a meal on their own. In southern India, thick rice dishes like Mango Rice (page 129) are popular. Northern basmati rice is often cooked with cardamom, cloves, and cinnamon, but sometimes to accompany a very flavorful dish a plainer preparation is preferable. For a dinner party, try making a colorful pilaf dome by using a bowl as a mold. With a bigger setting you can actually make two pilafs and layer them in the mold. Choose two with distinct colors and taste like Red Pepper and Tomato (page 130) with Apple Mustard Rice (page 125). You can even cheat if you want and add a little food color to enhance the result.

Couscous is the national dish of Morocco. Strictly speaking it's not a whole grain but tiny pieces of pasta, which is prepared by carefully steaming and raking. Great pride is taken in the lightness of the finished dish. It is accompanied by a stew, which was part of the steaming process but here I have opted to present a less labor-intensive option using instant couscous (page 127). Don't feel restricted to a given recipe with couscous. A great idea is to spread out couscous on a large platter and then lay out skewered barbecued vegetables on top. You can expand that idea and host a mini buffet right on the couscous with Lima Bean Patties (page 109) and Stuffed Peppers (page 87) along with the barbecued vegetables. Remember to include a salad alongside, like Moroccan Green Pepper Salad (page 140) or Moroccan Orange and Black Olive Salad (page 141). A spicy Za'atar (page 146) or Harissa dip (page 155) would be a good addition for the fire-eaters.

Apple Mustard Rice

Type: South Indian
Preparation: 30 minutes soaking
Speed: Less than an hour
Notes: This dish is pretty filling, so you might want to eat it just with some soup.

- 1 cup basmati rice
- 1 teaspoon salt
- 1 teaspoon plus 1 teaspoon black mustard seeds
- ½ teaspoon asafetida
- 6 fresh red chiles
- ¼ cup desiccated coconut
- ½ teaspoon ground turmeric

- 2 large cooking apples, peeled, cored, and cut into ½-inch pieces
- 3 tablespoons oil
- 1 tablespoon dry chana dal
- 1 whole fresh green chile
- 8 curry leaves
- ¼ cup raw shelled peanuts
- 6 more curry leaves

Soak the rice for half an hour, covered by about an inch of water, and then bring to a boil. Lower the heat, add the salt, and simmer until rice is cooked, less than 20 minutes. Add a little more water if needed. Let the pan stand undisturbed. Crush the first teaspoon of mustard seeds with a mortar and pestle, then put it into a food processor with the asafetida, chiles, coconut, turmeric, and half the apple. Blend to a paste.

Heat oil in a skillet. Once the oil is hot, add another teaspoon of mustard seed and the dal. When the mustard seeds crack, add the chile, curry leaves, and peanuts. The raw dal must be cooked through before continuing. Add the remaining apple pieces. Take care not to burn these ingredients. Once the apple is cooked through but still firm, add the contents of the processor and cook stirring continually for 5 minutes. Carefully fold the mixture into the rice, add the remaining curry leaves, then serve warm or at room temperature.

Grains

Basmati Northern Style

Type: North Indian
Preparation: ½ hour soaking
Speed: ½ hour
Notes: This flavored rice is a good accompaniment to most North Indian food.

- 1 cup basmati rice
- 1½ cups water
- 2 teaspoons salt
- 1 stick cassia or cinnamon

- 3 cardamom pods, very lightly crushed
- 5 whole cloves

Soak all ingredients together for 30 minutes. It is not necessary to rinse the rice first. Bring the pot to a boil, turn the heat down to low, cover, and simmer for about 20 minutes until the water has evaporated. Check to ensure the rice does not burn. Do not stir, but remove it from the heat and let stand for 5 minutes. Fluff it and turn into a serving bowl.

Option: You can bolster this rice while at the same time adding color by adding ⅓ cup of peas toward the end of cooking.

Grains

Couscous

Type: Moroccan
Preparation: You will need vegetable stock (page 17)
Speed: Very fast
Notes: Historically, couscous was made from the core of the grain that resisted the grinder. These days we have instant couscous easily available. The instant variety has been presteamed so you don't need to use the traditional couscous steamer. This special pot, however, does impart the flavor of the boiling stew in the lower chamber to the couscous above. In this quick and easy recipe I use vegetable stock to preload the flavor. Couscous should be light and fluffy, not stodgy. Use it as a bed for Black Vegetable Medley (page 223), Eggplant and Chickpeas (page 100), or a nest for Tomato-Stuffed Eggplant (page 120).

- 2 cups instant couscous
- 1 teaspoon salt
- 1 large pinch saffron strands
- 2½ cups vegetable stock (page 17)
- 1 tablespoon olive oil

Place the couscous in a bowl with the salt and saffron. Bring the stock to a boil and pour it over the couscous and quickly stir in the olive oil. Let it sit covered for about 7 or 8 minutes, then fluff it up and serve.

Grains

127

Lime Rice Pilaf

Type: South Indian
Preparation: Make the rice the day before and soak the split peas overnight
Speed: Fast
Notes: This dish is good hot, but even better the next day cold.

- 2 cups basmati rice (prepare the day before)
- 2½ cups water
- ½ cup yellow split peas
- 3 teaspoons salt
- ¼ cup oil
- ½ teaspoon black mustard seeds
- 12 dry red chiles (stalks removed)
- 1 teaspoon asafetida
- 1 tablespoon lime peel, grated
- 3 tablespoons ginger
- 1½ teaspoon turmeric
- 1 teaspoon cayenne pepper
- ½ cup lime juice
- 10 curry leaves
- ½ cup cashews
- 3 slices of lime for garnish

Grains

Prepare the rice and split peas the day before, or in the morning for an evening meal. Soak the rice in the water for 30 minutes. Add the salt and bring to a boil, then simmer on low heat for about 15 minutes. Do not stir but check that the rice has not dried out prematurely. If it has dried out, dribble a little extra water in without disturbing the rice. Once it has fully cooked, remove from the heat and let stand until it is cold. Gently fluff the rice, trying not to break the grain, move into a bowl, and refrigerate until the next day. You should have 3 to 3½ cups. Rinse split peas until the water runs clear, then cover them with water in a container and soak overnight.

The next day, rinse and then spread the split peas on a paper towel and thoroughly dry them. Heat the oil in a large skillet and add the mustard seeds. As they start popping, add the split peas stirring over medium heat. After a few minutes they will darken a little. Make sure to keep stirring to prevent burning. Turn the heat to low and add the peppers, stir quickly, and add the asafetida. After the asafetida sizzles for just a second, add the lime peel, ginger, turmeric, and cayenne pepper. Mix the spices, then add the lime juice and curry leaves. Blend well and sprinkle on the rice. Cover and cook over low heat for 5 minutes, mixing often, while being careful not to break up the rice. Switch off the heat and let stand for a few minutes while you dry roast the cashews in a pan. They should not burn but just start to get darker patches. Carefully mix in the cashews, turn onto a serving plate, and garnish with the slices of fresh lime.

Mango Rice

Type: South Indian
Preparation: Overnight soaking
Speed: About an hour
Notes: This rice dish is filling on its own. Serve with a little Rasam (page 50-51) and chutney.

- ¼ cup yellow split peas
- 1½ cups basmati rice
- 2 cups water
- 1 large firm mango, not quite ripe
- ¼ cup desiccated coconut
- 1 teaspoon coriander seeds
- 1 teaspoon asafetida
- 1 teaspoon turmeric
- 1 teaspoon cayenne pepper
- 1 tablespoon salt
- ¼ cup oil
- 1½ teaspoon black mustard seeds
- ½ teaspoon cumin seeds
- 2 dry red chile peppers
- 20 fresh curry leaves

Soak the split peas overnight in enough water to cover. Soak the rice in water for 30 minutes. Peel and chop the mango into small cubes. You should have about 2 cups or a pound after the pit is discarded.

Dry roast the coconut and coriander seeds until it is an even cinnamon color, then grind them in a spice grinder. Transfer the mixture into a food processor and add the asafetida, turmeric, cayenne, and a cup of the chopped mango. Process to a paste and set aside in a small bowl.

Bring the rice to a boil with the salt, cover, and then simmer until the rice is cooked and the water has evaporated. Let the rice sit in a bowl until it is cold.

Drain and dry the split peas. Heat the oil in a skillet and fry the mustard and cumin seeds until they start to spit. Add the split peas and fry until they are golden brown and cooked through, making sure not to burn them. Add the red peppers and the curry leaves while stirring. Once the peppers turn a shade darker, add the remaining chopped mango. Fry for about 5 minutes, then add the paste. Continue frying for another 5 minutes. Mix the fried ingredients into the rice. You can eat this rice hot or cold.

Grains

Red Pepper and Tomato Pilaf

Type: Indian
Preparation: Make the rice and fire roast the red bell pepper several hours ahead of time
Speed: ½ hour
Notes: The nigella seeds impart a distinctive flavor to this pilaf.

- 2 cups basmati rice
- 1 tablespoon salt
- 1 stick cinnamon
- 1 tablespoon oil
- 1 tablespoon coconut oil
- 1 teaspoon cumin seeds
- 1 teaspoon black onion (nigella) seeds
- 4 whole cloves
- 1 medium onion, chopped
- 1 tablespoon chopped ginger
- 1 clove garlic, finely chopped
- 1 large tomato, peeled and finely chopped
- ½ teaspoon cayenne pepper
- 1 large fire-roasted red bell pepper (about 3 ounces after prep), chopped

Cover the rice with water and let sit for half an hour with the salt and cinnamon.

Bring the pot to a boil and simmer for about 10 minutes. Let it stand in the saucepan until it cools. Remove to a covered bowl and let it stand for several hours.

Heat the oils in a skillet. Once hot, add the cumin and onion seeds. Let them sizzle for a few seconds, then add the cloves, onion, ginger, and garlic. Fry for about 8 minutes until the onion is cooked. Stir in the tomato and cayenne, then fry until the tomato is assimilated into the onion mix, about 5 minutes. Add the red pepper, stir, cover, and cook on low heat for 5 minutes. Now stir the mixture into the rice. Turn the rice into a large saucepan and warm though before serving.

Grains

> **Option:** One serving idea is to pack the finished rice into a bowl, then place a decorative plate over it and invert it. Remove the bowl to leave an attractive rice dome.

Rice Pilaf

Type: North Indian
Speed: Less than an hour
Notes: This pilaf has a glazed finish and is colorful and filling.

- 3 tablespoons coconut oil
- 1 tablespoon oil
- ½ teaspoon carom seeds
- 1 teaspoon cumin seeds
- 2 whole cloves
- 2 cardamom pods
- 10 bay leaves (fresh if available)
- 2 cups basmati rice
- 2 cups water
- 1½ teaspoons salt
- 1 scallion, chopped
- ¼ cup frozen peas, defrosted

Heat the oils in a saucepan. Add the carom, cumin, cloves, and cardamom. Let sizzle for a few seconds, add the bay leaves, stir, and immediately remove from the heat. Add rice, water, salt, and scallion. Let stand covered for 30 minutes.

Bring to a boil, cover, and simmer for about 10 minutes on low heat. Fold in the defrosted peas and heat through for a minute or so. Remove from the heat and let stand for 5 minutes before fluffing up and transferring to a serving bowl.

Grains

Toasted Coconut Rice

Type: South Indian
Preparation: ½ hour soaking
Speed: About 30 minutes
Notes: South Indian cuisine has a continuum of textures, particularly with regards to moisture. Dishes range form very thin pepper water through soups, sambars, gravies, dry preparations, and believe it or not, powders. This dish is very dry and should accompany a moist dish like Sambar (page 78) or curry. Being flavorful, this rice works well with a simple dal.

- 2 cups basmati rice
- 3 cups water
- 1 teaspoon coriander seeds
- ½ cup desiccated coconut
- ¼ cup sesame seeds
- 2 tablespoons white poppy seeds
- 1 teaspoon turmeric
- ¼ teaspoon cayenne pepper
- 1 teaspoon salt

- 1 tablespoon oil
- 1 teaspoon black mustard seeds
- ½ teaspoon cumin
- 1 teaspoon urad dal
- ½ teaspoon asafetida
- 10 curry leaves
- 2 dry red chile peppers
- 2 tablespoons lemon juice

Grains

Cover the rice with water and let sit for 30 minutes. Dry roast the coriander, coconut, sesame, and poppy seeds until they are an even cinnamon color. Grind to a powder in a spice grinder, then move to a bowl and add the turmeric, cayenne, and salt. Mix to eliminate any lumps. Bring the rice to a boil, then reduce to a low simmer and cover with the lid slightly ajar. After about 15 minutes the rice should be cooked and the water evaporated. Without stirring, let the rice stand for 5 minutes. Carefully mix in the spice powder and let stand covered.

Heat the oil in a skillet and add the mustard, cumin, and urad dal. When the mustard is popping add the asafetida, curry leaves, and peppers. Once the peppers darken, fold the contents into the cooked rice and add the lemon juice. Now return the saucepan to low heat for another 5 minutes before serving.

One Potato, Two Potato

Salads didn't really figure very highly when I was growing up in rural England. We ate a rotation of Brit favorites: chips (fries), beans on toast, Marmite on toast, and the lavish Sunday dinner, but even this traditional feast rarely boasted anything green save peas or runner beans.

In turn, both of my brothers and I worked at the local fish and chip shop preparing the potatoes. The volume of chips consumed from this small village shop was incredible. After school on Friday night I would don an apron and set to work in the outbuildings behind the shop. Fortunately, I didn't have to touch any fish—that was prepared in the main shop front—but I was responsible for heaving 56-pound bags of King Edward potatoes into the peeling machine. Perhaps it is my imagination, but to this day the outer side of my right index finger feels like it has slightly toughened skin where the knife was gripped as I removed the defects in the potatoes. On Fridays alone, apparently a big chip night in the '70s, I would prepare ten or more huge waist-high plastic drums of chips ready for the fryer. This volume was almost the same on Saturday when it was common for the locals to eat fish and chips for lunch. I didn't eat fish but ate chips with beans or the curry sauce that was made entirely from a pre-prepared powder and water. Again there was nothing green to be seen, except the mushy peas boiling away in the back, and that was only green courtesy of a dye called "Pea Green."

The idea of eating salad came much later for me, particularly when elements can be grown in the garden. I like mâche (also known as lamb's lettuce or field salad) very much, and once I decide to make hummus or baba ghanoush a salad now seems essential.

Salads & Dressings

When most people hear the word "vegan," they think of salads, usually followed by "I couldn't be a vegan" or "I need meat," etc. I can almost agree. That is, if you think that all a vegan can eat is raw vegetables and your definition of a salad is the mainstream notion based on lettuce and tomato. This, however, is a straw-man argument because around the world a salad is rarely just lettuce and tomato with a vinegar/oil dressing. In fact salads can be quite diverse and interesting. Sometimes they are even served hot. There are fruit salads, vegetable salads, bound salads, pasta salads, and that's just a few of the vegetarian options. Salads from regions around the world challenge the conventional Western concept of what a salad is.

The other half of the equation, the dressing, can be equally varied. Virgin olive oil and lemon juice works well enough for some salads, but generally I prefer a more robust option. Taratoor (Sesame Sauce) (page 146) is a favorite of mine, as is Ajvar (page 137). Both can double as falafel dressing and both bind well to the salad, avoiding the awful dressing pool at the bottom of the bowl, which you often see with the thinner dressings. Generally, I like to serve the salad and dressing separately so people have options and the greens don't wilt.

In the Recycled section
Miner's Lettuce Salad (page 228)

Ajvar

Type: Balkan/Turkish
Preparation: You will need 1½ cups of fire-roasted, skinned red bell pepper and a cup of fire-roasted eggplant (page 15)
Speed: Less than an hour
Notes: Numerous variations of Ajvar (vegan caviar) can be found across the Balkans and Turkey but the key ingredients are always peppers and eggplant. It's eaten as a dip with bread but can be used as a salad dressing, topping for Hummus (page 70), or a base source for a bowl of mixed olives. Ajvar is made sweet or spicy—this can be achieved by using spicy peppers but here I included an option to heat it up a little by the addition of chili powder. This can be increased if you want a fiery ajvar.

- 1½ cup fire-roasted red bell pepper
- 1 cup fire-roasted eggplant pulp
- ¼ Preserved Lemon (page 165), chopped
- 2 large cloves garlic, minced
- 1 teaspoon salt
- ½ teaspoon chili powder (optional)
- ⅛ teaspoon freshly ground black pepper
- ¼ cup olive oil

Mince the peppers and eggplant in a food processor with the preserved lemon. Then put the mixture into a saucepan with the garlic, salt, chili powder, and ground pepper. Bring to a boil, then simmer for half an hour to reduce the liquid. Return to the processor and process again, adding the olive oil, until it is evenly processed. Put into a sterilized jar and store in the refrigerator. Serve cold as a dip with pita bread, garnished with chopped parsley or pine nuts.

Salads & Dressings

Barbecue Sauce

Type: Arabian
Speed: Very fast
Notes: All over the Middle East, a wide variety of foods are barbecued. Here is a barbecue sauce, which will work great with corn on the cob, shallots, and other vegetables.

- ¼ cup olive oil
- 2 cloves garlic
- 1 tablespoon fresh oregano
- 1 tablespoon fresh thyme
- 1 tablespoon fresh parsley

- 1 tablespoon paprika
- ½ teaspoon salt
- 1 ounce oil-cured black olives (pitted)
- 1 small tomato, chopped

Blend all ingredients in a food processor or a blender until you have a sauce that retains some texture (do not overblend).

Black Olive Sauce

Type: Arabian
Speed: Less than an hour
Notes: This sauce can be used raw as a grilling sauce for corn. Simply coat the ears generously and grill. To get that flame-kissed taste, don't wrap in tinfoil; the sauce will keep the corn moist. This sauce can also be used, after frying, as a pesto.

Salads & Dressings

- 2 tablespoons (packed) fresh parsley, chopped
- 2 tablespoons (packed) fresh oregano, chopped
- 1 teaspoon (packed) fresh tender thyme
- ½ small Preserved Lemon (page 165)
- 3 cloves garlic

- 2 ounces pitted, oil-cured black olives
- ¼ cup olive oil
- 1 teaspoon paprika
- 1 tablespoon tomato paste
- ¼ teaspoon Harissa (page 155) (optional)
- ½ teaspoon salt

Discard the thick stems of the herbs and chop. Blend all the ingredients together into a paste in a food processor. It is ready to use as a grilling sauce, but for a pasta sauce or flavoring for salad or vegetables, fry the sauce for 3 minutes, stirring constantly to cook the garlic through.

Cucumber Salad

Type: Arabian
Speed: Fast
Notes: Persian seedless cucumbers are perfect for this dish, but English seedless cucumbers would also work. Serve this fresh before the cucumbers go limp.

- 6 smallish Persian cucumbers (about 1 pound)
- 2 scallions, diced
- 2 packed tablespoons chopped fresh dill
- 2 tablespoons olive oil
- 2 tablespoons orange juice
- 1 tablespoon lemon juice
- 1 teaspoon sumac powder
- ¼ teaspoon salt
- 4 black peppercorns, ground
- Fresh mint for garnish

Trim the ends of the cucumbers and cut into thin rounds. Lay them out on a paper towel while you chop the scallions and dill. Mix the oil, orange juice, lemon juice, sumac, salt, and pepper together to form a dressing. In a bowl, mix the cucumber, scallions, dill, and dressing. Toss until the cucumbers are well coated, serve in a shallow bowl, and garnish with a few mint leaves.

Salads & Dressings

139

Lebanese Salad

Type: Lebanese
Speed: Fast
Notes: This salad goes well as a side dish to Spinach Pies (page 37).

- 1 small cucumber
- ½ red bell pepper
- 2 medium tomatoes
- 4 scallions
- 2 tablespoons chopped parsley
- 2 tablespoons chopped mint
- 2 tablespoons chopped cilantro
- ¼ cup olive oil
- Juice from 1 lemon
- ½ teaspoon salt
- ⅛ teaspoon ground black pepper

Trim away the cucumber skin and slice into thin rounds. Discard the seeds and stem of the pepper and dice into pieces about the size of a fingernail. Dice the tomatoes and cut the scallions into thin rounds. Place everything into a bowl.

In a food processor, make a dressing out of the parsley, mint, cilantro, oil, lemon juice, salt, and pepper. Make sure it is fully processed before stirring it into the bowl. Refrigerate until serving, but it is best served right away, before the cucumber goes limp.

Moroccan Green Pepper Salad

Salads & Dressings

Type: Moroccan
Preparation: You will need 2 fire-roasted green bell peppers
Speed: Fast
Notes: There are many versions of this salad in Morocco. It is a refreshing dish for a light summer meal.

- 2 large fire-roasted green bell peppers
- 3 large tomatoes
- ¼ teaspoon black pepper
- Pinch of celery seeds
- Pinch of dill seeds
- ¼ teaspoon ground cumin
- ½ teaspoon salt
- ¼ teaspoon paprika
- ¼ small Preserved Lemon (page 165), chopped
- 2 tablespoons olive oil
- 1 tablespoon lemon juice

Roast the peppers (page 16) deseed, remove the skin, core, and stem. Cut the peppers into strips about 1½ inches by ¾ inch and set aside on a paper towel. Cut the tomatoes into segments and place in a bowl. While the peppers cool, make the dressing.

Using a mortar and pestle, grind the black pepper, celery seeds, and dill seeds to a fine powder. Add the cumin, salt, paprika, and preserved lemon, and pound to a paste. Add the oil and lemon juice to the paste and stir in with a spoon.

Now combine the tomatoes, peppers, and dressing in a mixing bowl. Serve.

Moroccan Orange and Black Olive Salad

Type: Moroccan
Speed: Fast
Notes: This is a most vivid salad. One idea is to use the olives to make a pattern between the oranges.

- 3 oranges
- 1 cup black olives (I prefer oil-cured in this dish)
- 2 tablespoons olive oil
- 2 medium cloves garlic, minced
- ⅛ teaspoon cayenne pepper
- ½ teaspoon paprika
- ½ teaspoon salt
- ⅛ teaspoon ground cumin
- 2 tablespoons parsley, finely chopped

Peel oranges and dress segments by removing the white membranes. Arrange the orange segments in a shallow decorative bowl. Pit the olives but keep them whole and arrange them artistically between the orange segments. Stir the other ingredients together in a small bowl, pour over the oranges and olives, and serve.

Salads & Dressings

141

North African Flavored Pasta Salad

Type: North African
Preparation: Fire roast onions and fennel bulbs
Speed: Fast
Notes: This is a hot salad that combines pasta and fire-roasted vegetables.

- 1 fire-roasted fennel bulb
- 2 medium fire-roasted onions
- 1 cup pasta (penne or shells work well)
- Salt
- 1 tablespoon olive oil
- ¼ teaspoon Preserved Lemon (page 165)
- 2 cloves garlic, minced
- ½ teaspoon Harissa (page 155) or cayenne pepper
- 1 tablespoon chopped fresh oregano
- 1 teaspoon paprika
- 1 medium tomato, coarsely chopped
- 10 oil-cured olives (pit them in advance)

Trim away the burnt layers of the fennel and onions and cut them into about 8 pieces each. Bring a saucepan of salt water to a boil and add the pasta. Reduce to medium heat and while it is simmering make a sauce in a small bowl with the olive oil, lemon, harissa, oregano, garlic, and paprika. Mix it all together with a fork. When the pasta is almost done (*al dente*) heat a skillet over medium heat and add the onion and fennel. Keep turning the vegetables until they are warmed through, then add the sauce. Stir for about a minute before adding the tomato. Drain the pasta in a colander. Stir the skillet until the tomato chunks go limp and are cooked through but still in one piece. Now add the pasta and olives. Fold over the mixture to ensure the pasta is coated with sauce, then serve hot in a shallow bowl.

Salads & Dressings

Pepper Sauce

Type: Arabian
Preparation: You can use premade Fire-Roasted Peppers (page 16)
Speed: Fast
Notes: You will need 3 to 4 red bell peppers (or for a colorful variation use yellow bell peppers). This sauce is a refreshing change from the usual tomato-based sauces over pasta. It makes a nice smoky salad dressing or a dip for chips. If you don't like too much heat, cut down the harissa or hot pepper by half.

- 10 ounces fire-roasted red bell peppers skinned (see Ganging Up, page 16)
- 1 red chile pepper (or ½ teaspoon Harissa, page 155)
- 3 cloves garlic
- 2 tablespoons olive oil

- ½ teaspoon salt
- 1 teaspoon chopped fresh oregano (or ½ teaspoon dry)
- 2 teaspoons chopped fresh parsley (reserve 1 teaspoon for garnish)
- ½ teaspoon za'atar

Blend all the ingredients in a food processor. In a skillet, heat the paste to dry it out a little. If you want to use the sauce for pasta, fry it until the garlic loses its raw smell, about 3 minutes. For a dip, I like to cook it a little longer until it stiffens up a little, then serve it in a bowl garnished with reserved parsley.

Salads & Dressings

143

Roasted Red Pepper Bulgur Salad

Type: Arabian
Speed: Fast
Notes: This salad makes a colorful side dish, or tasty cordon around a vegetable dish like Tomato-Stuffed Eggplant (page 120). A second option is to use it to stuff tomatoes for easy finger food at a party.

- 1 cup bulgur
- ¾ cup boiling water
- 2 fire-roasted red bell peppers (page 16)
- Juice from 2 lemons
- ¼ Preserved Lemon (page 165)
- 1 teaspoon salt
- 4 scallions
- 1 small bunch of parsley (about ¼ cup once trimmed)
- 1 bunch of fresh mint (about ¼ cup once trimmed)
- 1 large tomato (unless stuffing tomatoes)
- ½ cup olive oil

Place the bulgur in a warm bowl and add boiling water. Stir, cover, and let stand for half an hour.

In a food processor, make a paste using one of the fire-roasted red peppers, lemon juice, preserved lemon, and salt.

Very finely chop the scallions, parsley, and mint (discarding the thick stalks) as well as the second fire-roasted pepper and the tomato.

Once the bulgur has soaked for half an hour, stir in the paste and chopped ingredients. Fold in the olive oil and refrigerate it until needed. The flavor and texture improve somewhat after it stands for a couple of hours.

Salads & Dressings

Option: To stuff small tomatoes, omit the tomato in the ingredient list. Select about 20 firm small ripe tomatoes, rinse and cut off the top portion, then scoop out the center using a knife and small teaspoon. Place the tomatoes upside down on the chopping board to drain while you finely dice the tomato centers and tops (discarding the hard stalk matter). Stir the chopped tomato into the bulgur.

Using your hands, pack each tomato with the bulgur salad. Arrange the stuffed tomatoes on a bed of lettuce or in a serving dish. Half-pitted black olives can be used as caps. I prefer to cap selectively to make a pattern across the top. Of course the smaller the tomatoes the more you will need.

Spicy Fava Bean Salad

Type: North African
Speed: ½ hour
Notes: Fava beans are quite flavorful, so I don't like to overpower them with too many ingredients, but combined just with this spicy sauce the beans will retain their flavor. You'll need around 4 pounds of fava beans to get the 1 pound of de-podded, skinned beans.

   If you want to up the heat factor a little, double the harissa. Once skinned, the fava beans have a rich green color and make an attractive side dish to Spinach Pies (page 37) or Falafel (page 101).

- 1 pound skinned fresh fava beans (about 4 pounds in the pod)
- 1 teaspoon fresh dill weed, finely chopped
- 1 teaspoon Harissa (page 155)
- 1 tablespoon olive oil
- 1 teaspoon za'atar

Select fava pods that bulge with large beans. Bring a pot of salt water to a boil while you harvest the beans from the pods. Skin the beans by boiling them for a few minutes and then squeezing off the skins. Keep the water in the saucepan and return the skinned beans. Boil for 5 minutes. Meanwhile, mix together the dill, harissa, olive oil, and za'atar to make a sauce. Drain the beans in a colander and return to the empty pan off the heat. Mix in the sauce until it is evenly distributed. Serve hot in a shallow bowl. Alternatively, cover the bowl with plastic, refrigerate, and eat them cold later.

Salads & Dressings

Taratoor (Sesame Sauce)

Type: Lebanese
Speed: Very fast
Notes: This is the classic dressing for falafel. It is also a rich option as a salad dressing.

- 3 cloves garlic, chopped
- 1 cup tahini
- 1 cup water
- ½ cup lemon juice
- ½ teaspoon salt

Blend all the ingredients in a food processor.

Za'atar Dip

Type: Lebanese
Speed: Very fast
Notes: One of the quickest snack dips out there. It is prepared from za'atar (a mixture often, but not always including sumac powder, sesame seeds, and powdered thyme) and oil. Za'atar is increasingly available in the U.S. and you are most likely to find it in Lebanese stores. You can brush this dip on bread before it is baked in the oven.

- 4 tablespoons za'atar
- 6 tablespoons olive oil

Mix to form a paste and eat as dip with pita bread.

Salads & Dressings

A Limey's Pickle

When I was returning to California from London, the customs officer asked me, "What's in the bag, Marmite and Branston pickle?" He was right, of course. The British Passport was a giveaway. Over the past few years I have lectured about various subjects related to science and belief. I was asked at one lecture what I thought the best evidence of the existence of God is. I don't find any compelling evidence but answered somewhat tongue-in-cheek, the music of J.S. Bach. I have no serious reason to invoke a deity, but in keeping with that light spirit, if such an entity did exist Marmite would be second on my list of proofs and the deity would surely be eating it. Like with durian in Malaysia, the big divide in Briton is between haters or lovers of the brown elixir. The company has even used this controversy in its advertising and sometimes runs ads showing people's disgust with their product.

Actually Marmite is not a pickle; it's an extract. Our national pickle is Branston pickle, used for ploughman's lunch and above all to insert in cheddar cheese sandwiches. Branston and cheddar go together in the UK like fries and ketchup in the U.S. Not apparently for my father, however, who stubbornly took plain cheese sandwiches to work for about 40 years. Mum would try to coax him with embellishments, to no avail.

Branston pickle consists of diced vegetables in a vinegar, tomato, apple, and date sauce with spices. It has a decidedly sweet/sour taste with crunchy pearl onions. Together with Marmite, thick-cut marmalade, and Colman's mustard, Branston pickle rescues the native food from otherwise total blandness. Marmite and Branston pickle have both been potato chip flavors in the UK; we can't get enough!

Pickles & Chutney

Clearly pickling is not only a way to preserve and stretch food sources beyond their season, but also provides a concentrate to flavor other volumes of food. In India, farm workers can have a midday meal of rice in the fields flavored only with a strong pickle. In Morocco, preserved lemons are an important ingredient in cooking, while in Lebanon a little pickle on the side transforms a dish of hummus to an attractive light meal. Whether traditionally developed to preserve food through the heat of the summer or the freezing winter, pickles can really add a tempting element to a meal.

For an Indian buffet, I like to set out a large *thali*-style selection of chutney and pickles in small bowls called *katoris*. For an Arabian buffet I sometimes present a bowl including mixed pickled vegetables with olives dressed with a little olive oil. Hot pickled peppers and preserved lemon slices add some zip. Don't rule out using a little pickled vegetable as a garnish for Fūl (page 104) or even a soup. For North African meals, I like to prepare a shallow bowl of olives and peppers in Ajvar (page 137) or Harissa (page 155) sauce.

In the Recycled section
Banana Peel Relish (page 221)
Lemon Peel and Onion Relish (page 227)
Nasturtium Seed Pickle (page 229)

Chile Citrus Pickle

Type: Indian
Speed: Less than an hour
Notes: This is a colorful version of a common hot Indian pickle. The small red chiles add a splash of color along with a blast of heat.

- 1½ pounds unblemished limes
- ¾ pound green chiles
- 2 medium lemons
- 20 small fresh Thai peppers
- 10 ounces fresh ginger, peeled
- ½ pound salt
- 1¾ cups oil
- 2 tablespoons carom seeds
- 2 tablespoons black cumin seeds
- 1 teaspoon asafetida
- 2 tablespoons turmeric

Wash and completely dry the limes and chiles. Cut the limes into 8 segments each, including the peel. Cut the green chiles into 1-inch barrels, removing the stalk end. Slice and remove seeds from the lemons, again including the peel. Keep the red chiles whole but remove the stems and slit lengthwise. Cut the ginger into small matchsticks. Place them all into a large bowl and add the salt. Toss the ingredients until completely coated in the salt. Set the bowl aside for half an hour.

Heat the oil in a large skillet. Meanwhile, mix the carom, cumin, asafetida, and turmeric in a bowl next to the skillet. When the oil is hot, add the spices, stir once, then add the citrus-chile mix immediately. Maintain a high heat and cook for about 8 minutes, mixing frequently. Prepare one or two sterilized jars large enough to hold the pickle. Spoon in the pickle and let it cool a little before sealing with a lid. Refrigerate. It will be ready in about 10 days and will keep for many months. It is important not to spoon out this type of pickle with a damp spoon, which will turn it moldy.

Pickles & Chutneys

Coconut Chutney #1

Type: South Indian
Speed: Less than an hour
Notes: Coconut chutney is a must for a southern Indian meal. This accompaniment traditionally sits on a banana leaf along with a pickle, rice, and perhaps Sambar (page 78). This version of coconut chutney uses dry-roasted urad dal for body.

- ¼ cup urad dal (rinsed and dried)
- ½ cup desiccated coconut
- 1 tablespoon cilantro leaves, chopped
- 3 green chiles, chopped and trimmed
- ¼ teaspoon salt
- ½ cup water
- 1 tablespoon lime juice
- 2 tablespoons oil
- 1 teaspoon black mustard seeds
- ½ teaspoon cumin seeds
- 1 dry red chile pepper
- ½ teaspoon asafetida
- 8 curry leaves

Dry roast the dal in an iron skillet. Move to a bowl and let it cool a little. Then grind to a powder in a spice grinder. Transfer the powder to a food processor. Add the coconut, cilantro, chiles, salt, water, and lime juice. Process to a paste, then empty the contents into a bowl.

Heat the oil in an iron skillet. Add the mustard and cumin seeds. Once they start popping add the pepper and the asafetida. Stir, then add the curry leaves. After they crackle, scrape the contents onto the mixture in the bowl. Fold in and serve.

Coconut Chutney #2

Type: South Indian
Speed: Less than an hour
Notes: This is a moister version that uses soy yogurt.

- 1 cup grated coconut
- ½ cup soy yogurt
- ¼ cup loosely packed cilantro leaves, chopped
- 2 green chiles
- ½ teaspoon salt
- 2 tablespoons water
- 3 tablespoons vegetable oil
- 1½ teaspoons black mustard seeds

Blend the first 6 ingredients in food processor until it becomes a smooth paste. Heat the oil in frying pan until hot, then add the mustard seeds. When they stop popping, scrape the contents onto the coconut paste, mix, and serve.

Fried Onion Garnish

Type: Indian
Speed: About an hour
Notes: It's a good idea to prepare this garnish when you are going to make a North Indian dish like Baingan Bharta (page 94) or Chana Masala (page 98). That way the oil can be shared without any clean-up. Aside from Indian dishes, this garnish is used in Canada as a hot dog condiment.

- 2 large onions, thinly sliced (about a pound after skinning and trimming)
- Oil for deep frying

Preheat the oven to 250ºF.

Put the onion slices on a baking tray in the oven for about 45 minutes.

Heat the oil in a skillet and fry the dehydrated onions for about 10 minutes while stirring. They should be a dark brown but not blackened. Remove the onion with a slotted spoon and refrigerate in an airtight container until needed.

Pickles & Chutneys

Fruit and Nut Chutney

Type: North Indian
Preparation: 1½ hours soaking
Speed: Less than 1½ hours
Notes: This chutney is very sweet, which goes well with North Indian dishes such as Chana Masala (page 98). Remember that it will thicken as it cools, so avoid cooking it until it becomes too stiff.

- 2 cups dried (unsulfured) Turkish apricots, chopped
- ½ cup dried (unsulfured) pineapple, chopped
- 5 dates, pitted and sliced
- ¼ cup raw almonds
- 4 cups boiling water
- ½ cup chopped fresh ginger
- ¼ cup garlic, chopped
- ⅓ cup plus 1 cup white wine vinegar
- 2 cups sugar
- ¼ teaspoon salt
- ½ teaspoon cayenne pepper
- ¾ cup golden raisins
- ½ cup currants
- ¼ teaspoon garam masala

Place the apricots, pineapple, dates, and almonds in a bowl and cover with the boiling water. Let sit for 1½ hours. Blend the ginger, garlic, and ⅓ cup of vinegar in the food processor to a paste. In a large pan, bring the remaining cup of vinegar, the garlic-ginger paste, and the soaking fruit and nuts to a boil. Add sugar, salt, and cayenne, then reduce the heat to a simmer. Simmer for half an hour, then add the raisins and currants. Stir frequently to avoid the bottom burning. Continue simmering on low heat for around 40 minutes. Again, do not let the bottom burn and watch the consistency. If it gets stiff, move straight on to the next stage. Add the garam masala and stir over low heat for another couple of minutes. Move into sterilized jars and cool with the lids off. Cover and keep in the refrigerator.

Pickles &
Chutneys

Harissa

Type: Arabian
Preparation: 1 hour soaking
Speed: Less than an hour (after soaking)
Notes: This recipe yields about a cup of harissa. One portion will easily supply enough paste to add to the recipes in this book, but it can also be served as a condiment or used as dip for bread. Spicy olive medleys often utilize a couple of tablespoons of harissa to add fire and taste.

- 2 cups dry red chile peppers, stalks removed
- 4 cups boiling water
- 2 tablespoons coriander seeds
- 1 tablespoon dried caraway seeds
- 8 medium cloves garlic, chopped
- 1 teaspoon salt
- ½ cup olive oil

Place the peppers in a bowl and pour on the boiling water. Let them soak for an hour. Meanwhile, dry roast the coriander and caraway seeds, then grind them to a powder in a spice grinder or mortar and pestle.

Drain the peppers and reserve the water for Indian Pepper Broth (page 233). Let the peppers drain in a colander for half an hour, shaking as much water from them as you can. Pat them dry with a paper towel and then add them to a food processor with the ground spices, garlic, salt, and olive oil. Blend to a paste. Sterilize a jar with boiling water, dry it completely, and then fill it with the harissa. Tap it down to get rid of any bubbles, then add a little more olive oil to seal it. Put on the lid and store in the refrigerator.

> **Option:** To make a dipping sauce from harissa paste mix 1 part harissa to 2 parts olive oil. You can also make a za'atar-harissa dip with equal parts harissa, za'atar, and olive oil. Remember that harissa is very hot. You'll need ample bread.

Pickles & Chutneys

Indian Vegetable Pickle

Type: Indian
Preparation: 5 days of standing time
Speed: This is a 5-day project
Notes: This is a mild, slightly sweet pickle, which can be made from any number of leftover raw vegetables.

- 1 pound mixed raw vegetables (for example carrots, onion, parsnips, peas, green beans)
- 3 cups water
- 3 large cloves garlic
- 1 small onion
- 1-inch piece fresh ginger
- ¼ cup vegetable oil
- 1 tablespoon yellow mustard seeds
- 1 teaspoon black cardamom seeds
- 1 teaspoon each red and black peppercorns
- ½ teaspoon cayenne pepper
- 1 teaspoon garam masala
- ½ teaspoon turmeric
- 2 tablespoons salt
- 5 tablespoons sugar
- 3 tablespoons vinegar

Cut the vegetables into 1-inch pieces. Bring water to a boil and boil the vegetables vigorously for a minute. Drain and place vegetables onto paper towels to dry.

Combine garlic, onion, and ginger with a little water in a food processor to make a paste. Heat oil and add paste and fry until golden. In a spice grinder, grind mustard, cardamom, and peppercorns to a powder. Place the pot over low heat and add the ground spices along with cayenne, garam masala, turmeric, and salt. Stir. Check that the vegetables are dry. If not, you can finish drying with a hair dryer. Add vegetables to the pot and fold until coated with spice mixture. Turn off the heat and spoon into a sterilized glass jar.

Leave the jar covered in direct sunlight for 2 days. Make sure the top is not sealed. You can use a piece of muslin between the lid and the jar to keep dust or insects from getting in but let vapor out.

Dissolve the sugar in boiling vinegar. Remove from heat and mix into the contents of the jar. Mix thoroughly and let stand for 3 days before using. Store in the refrigerator. It should be good for a few months.

Kiwi Chutney

Type: South Indian
Speed: Fast
Notes: This chutney is quite spicy and a little goes a long way. It goes well with Peanut Vada (page 74).

- 1 pound kiwis, peeled
- 1 tablespoon lime juice
- 1 tablespoon salt
- 1 teaspoon turmeric powder
- 2 tablespoons cayenne pepper

- 1 teaspoon asafetida
- 1 teaspoon fenugreek powder
- ½ cup vegetable oil
- 1 teaspoon black mustard seeds

In a food processor, mince the kiwis, lime juice, and salt. Mix the dry spices (except the black mustard seeds) in a small bowl. Heat the oil and then add the black mustard seeds. Once they start popping, stir in the spice mix quickly followed by the kiwi paste. Simmer on medium high heat for 15 minutes, then move into sterilized jars. It is ready as soon as it is cool. Refrigerated, it will keep a few weeks, but not as long as vinegar- or sugar-based chutneys.

Pickles &
Chutneys

Lime Pickle

Type: Indian
Preparation: Days of soaking and resting time
Speed: It will be more than 3 weeks before this pickle is ready
Notes: Often lemon and lime trees produce a quantity of small, underdeveloped fruit. They sometimes grow on the woody interior of older trees particularly when the tree is receiving insufficient light. Apart from perhaps slicing them for drinks they are usually left to rot on the tree or the ground. They are perfect to use in this highly spiced Indian pickle. Naturally, full-sized fruit works just as well, but it's a nice way to clear a tree of unwanted dwarf fruits. Pick only unblemished fruit. Notice that the recipe calls for yellow mustard powder. That does not refer to Colman's English mustard powder, or other similar brands, but rather ground yellow mustard seeds.

- 1½ pounds limes
- ½ cup salt
- ½ cup chili powder
- 1 tablespoon turmeric powder
- 2 tablespoons fenugreek powder
- ½ teaspoon asafetida
- 3 tablespoons yellow mustard powder
- 2½ tablespoons tablespoon ginger powder
- 1¼ cups vegetable oil

Wash and dry the limes fully. Cut limes less than an inch in diameter in half. Quarter or cut into 8 pieces the larger limes. Remove any seeds and then place them in clean dry bowl. Fold in salt and coat the lime pieces, then scoop into a large sterilized mason jar. Close the top (without rubber seal) and leave on a shelf or warm area for 10 days, shaking every morning.

Mix together the chili powder, turmeric, fenugreek, mustard, and ginger powder. Toss the salted limes in spice mixture, return to the jar, and leave to rest covered for 2 days.

Heat the oil on high and then add the asafetida, followed immediately by the spiced limes. Toss in hot oil for a minute before spooning the mixture into sterilized jars. Cool with the lids off. Once cool, cap (with recycled jars cover with a square of plastic wrap before screwing on the lid). The pickle is ready in about 10 days and will keep for many months.

Pickles & Chutneys

Longan and Onion Chutney

Type: Indian
Speed: About an hour
Notes: Longans, not to be confused with loganberries, look somewhat like lychees. Look for the fruit in Chinese grocery stores. This unusual sweet chutney has a fruity and caramelized onion taste and works well as an accompaniment for Samosas (page 39) or Pakoras (page 232). You can halve the cayenne to make it a little milder if you wish.

- 1 pound longans (after peeling and removing the stones)
- 1 tablespoon oil
- 1 teaspoon black mustard seeds
- ½ teaspoon asafetida
- 3 tablespoons finely chopped fresh ginger
- 2 onions, finely chopped

- 1 cup white wine vinegar
- 1 teaspoon salt
- ½ teaspoon turmeric powder
- 1 teaspoon cayenne pepper
- 1 teaspoon fenugreek powder
- 1 cup sugar
- 1 lemon, juiced and rind grated

Heat the oil in a saucepan and add the mustard seeds. When they start popping add the asafetida. Immediately after it sizzles, add the ginger and onions. Stir quickly and then add the vinegar, prepared longans, salt, turmeric, cayenne, fenugreek, sugar, lemon juice, and rind. Bring the pot to a boil, then reduce and simmer uncovered for 30 minutes. Cover the pan and continue to simmer for 10 minutes, stirring frequently. The chutney should now take on a thick, glazed look.

Sterilize a jar with boiling water and dry it completely. Spoon in the chutney, cap, and store the jar in a cupboard. It is ready the next day. After opening, store it in the refrigerator.

Pickles & Chutneys

Lotus Root and Date Chutney

Type: Indian
Speed: Less than an hour
Notes: This chutney is exceedingly sweet with an almost licorice taste. The trick is knowing when to stop cooking. With the unknown factors such as type of pan, exact heat, etc. it's best to judge on the constancy toward the end of the cooking process. I like to use black abbada dates to increase the licorice flavor, but medjool dates are very good too.

- 1 pound lotus roots
- 1 teaspoon black mustard seeds
- 1 teaspoon coriander seeds
- 1 teaspoon fennel seeds
- ½ teaspoon fenugreek seeds
- 1½ cups water

- ½ pound sugar
- ¼ cup coarsely chopped ginger
- ½ cup dates, diced
- 1 teaspoon salt
- ½ teaspoon cayenne pepper
- ⅛ teaspoon turmeric

Scrape the lotus roots and cut into ¼-inch wheels. Cut the bigger wheels into wedges like tiny pizza slices and the smaller ones in halves or leave whole. Store them in a bowl of water until needed. Dry roast black mustard, coriander, fennel, and fenugreek seeds in a small pan and grind to a powder in a spice grinder.

Boil the water and dissolve the sugar. Add the (drained) lotus root, ginger, dates, and salt. Continue to boil on medium heat for about 20 minutes. Stir often in the last 10 minutes to avoid burning. Add the remaining spices and stir until it is fully mixed. Carefully simmer until the liquid becomes slightly thick like honey. Remember, this type of high-sugar content chutney will thicken somewhat once cool. This should take about 15 minutes.

Put into a sterilized jar. Let the chutney cool with the lid open until barely warm. Close and keep in the refrigerator. This pickle is ready as soon as it has cooled but it doesn't keep as well as many other pickles—about 2 weeks.

Pickles & Chutneys

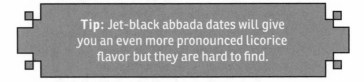

Tip: Jet-black abbada dates will give you an even more pronounced licorice flavor but they are hard to find.

Mint Chutney

Type: Indian
Speed: Very fast
Notes: This fresh, cold chutney, sometimes made with a mixture of mint and cilantro, has become a staple of the Indian restaurant starter plate along with papadoms.

- 1 cup loosely packed mint leaves
- 1 small onion, chopped
- Juice from one small lemon
- 1 green chile, seeded and chopped
- 1 tablespoon chopped ginger
- 3 large dates, pitted and chopped
- ¼ teaspoon salt
- ¼ teaspoon ground cumin

Place all the ingredients in a food processor and purée to an even paste.

Pickles & Chutneys

Orange and Almond Anglo-Indian Marmalade

Type: Anglo-Indian
Preparation: 1½ hours soaking
Speed: About 1½ hours
Notes: This marmalade is rather like very bitter traditional English thick-cut but with added Indian flavors. Remember that it will thicken once cool so avoid cooking it until it becomes too stiff. It is key to use bitter Seville oranges. If you can't find them dried, you can perhaps dehydrate them yourself or use another variety of bitter oranges.

- 4 ounces dried (unsulphered) Seville oranges, cut into ¼-inch bits
- 1 ounce raw almonds
- 2 cups boiling water
- 2 ounces chopped ginger
- 1 ounce garlic, chopped
- ¾ cup plus 1 cup white wine vinegar
- 1 cup sugar
- Pinch of salt
- ⅛ teaspoon cayenne pepper
- 2 ounces golden raisins
- ¼ teaspoon garam masala
- ¼ teaspoon ground cloves

Place the oranges and almonds in a bowl and cover with the boiling water. Let sit for 1½ hours. Process the ginger, garlic, and ¾ cup vinegar in the food processor to a paste. In a large pan, bring the remaining cup of vinegar, garlic-ginger paste, and soaked fruit and nuts (with the water) to a boil. Add sugar, salt, and cayenne and then reduce the heat to a simmer. Simmer on low heat for half an hour, then add the raisins. Continue simmering on low heat for 50 to 60 minutes. Do not let the bottom burn and watch the consistency. When it starts to get stiff, add the garam masala and ground cloves, then stir over low heat for another couple of minutes. Place into a sterilized jar and let the marmalade cool with the lid off. Cover and keep in the refrigerator.

Pickles & Chutneys

Options: I'm sure many Brits like me will be happy to eat this on toast like thick-cut marmalade, but you can also eat it as chutney with an Indian meal.

Pickled Vegetables

Type: Arabian
Speed: Fast
Notes: It's handy to have some pickled vegetables around to enhance a salad or a sandwich. The vegetables below are a suggestion but you can substitute your own, such as cucumber, golden beets, or turnip. The mace pieces, also called blades, are a staple in many picking spice mixtures but can be omitted if they are unavailable.

- ½ pound carrot, cut into ¾-inch chunks
- 1½ pounds cauliflower, broken into florets.
- ½ pound small onions or shallots
- 1 red bell pepper, seeded and cut into strips
- 3 cups water
- 1 tablespoon salt

- 6 cups apple cider vinegar
- 1 cinnamon stick
- 1 tablespoon yellow mustard seeds
- 2 teaspoons black peppercorns
- 1 teaspoon whole cloves
- 1 teaspoon whole allspice
- 1 teaspoon mace pieces
- 3 bay leaves
- 4 cloves garlic, sliced

Wash and prepare the vegetables. Peel the onions. Boil the water and dissolve the salt in it. Remove the pan from the heat and add vinegar.

Arrange the vegetables in a sterilized large glass jar, then place on top the cinnamon, mustard seeds, peppercorns, cloves, allspice, mace, bay leaves, and garlic. Pour on the water-vinegar mixture, which will carry some of the spices downward.

Close the lid and keep for 3 weeks on a shelf. After reopening, keep the jar in the refrigerator.

Pickles &
Chutneys

Pineapple and Date Chutney

Type: South Indian
Speed: About 30 minutes
Notes: This sweet chutney is very colorful and goes well with Peanut Vada (page 74) or koftas (pages 85, 110, and 119). It can be kept a few days in the refrigerator.

- Flesh from 1 mid-sized pineapple
- 1 tablespoon oil
- 2 tablespoons coconut oil
- 1 cinnamon stick
- ½ teaspoon cumin seeds
- ½ teaspoon fennel seeds
- 2 dry red chile peppers
- ¼ teaspoon ground cloves
- Seeds from 6 cardamom pods, crushed
- ¼ teaspoon cayenne pepper
- 1 tablespoon finely chopped fresh ginger
- 6 large dates, pitted and chopped
- 1 lemon, juiced
- ¼ cup sugar

Dice the pineapple into small chunks. Heat the oils in a large saucepan. Add the cinnamon, cumin, fennel, and peppers. Once the cumin darkens a shade, after a few seconds, add the ground cloves, cardamom, cayenne, and ginger. Stir and immediately add the pineapple chunks and dates.

Cover and cook on low heat until the pineapple is completely tender, about 15 minutes, but make sure the bottom of the pan is not burning by occasionally stirring. Add the lemon juice and increase the heat. Mix in the sugar and continue to cook while stirring for 5 more minutes. It will take on a glazed appearance and thicken. Serve warm or at room temperature, but if you keep the chutney in the refrigerator it's best to warm it up before eating, as the coconut oil can solidify.

Pickles &
Chutneys

Preserved Lemons

Type: Moroccan
Speed: Less than an hour
Notes: Preserved lemons are used in many Moroccan dishes. Wedges are added to bowls of pickles or olives, they are used in soup, and also add a nice flavor to a salad. It is my secret ingredient in hummus and baba ghanoush.

- Small lemons
- Salt

Wash and thoroughly dry the lemons. Prepare a sterilized jar. Trim away the stem end of each lemon and reserve any lemons with blemishes. Take the first lemon and cut it ⅘ of the way lengthwise, almost halving it. Turn it upside down and do the same thing again from the other end at right angles to the first cut. Sprinkle about ¼ teaspoon of salt inside each cut, then place the lemon in the jar. Continue this procedure until the jar is full, adding a little salt on each layer. The lemons will release some juice. Squeeze the juice from the rejected lemons until the salted lemons are covered. Store for 3 months before using.

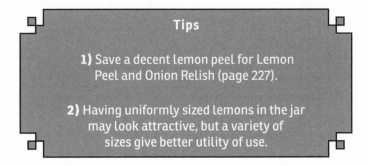

Tips

1) Save a decent lemon peel for Lemon Peel and Onion Relish (page 227).

2) Having uniformly sized lemons in the jar may look attractive, but a variety of sizes give better utility of use.

Pickles & Chutneys

Sweet Garlic and Chile Pickle

Type: Indian
Preparation: If short on time, the paste can be prepared ahead
Speed: Less than an hour
Notes: Select chiles according to your taste for heat and choose one garlic bulb with an abundance of small cloves.

- 2 bulbs garlic, about 4 ounces
- 1 pound green chile peppers
- ¼ cup yellow mustard seeds
- ¼ cup cumin seeds
- 1 teaspoon fenugreek seeds
- 1 teaspoon carom seeds

- 3 tablespoons turmeric
- ¼ teaspoon asafetida
- 1 cup white wine vinegar
- ½ cup sugar
- 1 tablespoon salt
- ⅔ cup vegetable oil

Break garlic into cloves, then trim and skin. Divide them into two equal piles by weight one with the smallest cloves and another the larger. Trim the stalk end of the chiles and cut them into ½-inch sections. Set them aside in a bowl with the smaller garlic cloves.

In a spice grinder, grind the mustard, cumin, fenugreek, and carom seeds to a powder. Put the powder into a food processor with turmeric, asafetida, vinegar, sugar, salt, and large garlic cloves. Process to a paste and set aside in a small bowl. Note: this stage can be done ahead of time, even the previous day, and left in the refrigerator.

Heat the oil in a skillet. Add the paste and fry, stirring for about 8 minutes on medium heat. The paste should then accept the oil. Add the small garlic cloves and chiles, keep mixing making sure the paste doesn't burn on the bottom. As the peppers get soft, be sure not to mash them. Boil water to sterilize a jar. After about 20 minutes, turn off the heat and spoon the pickle into the dry, sterilized jar.

Leave the lid off until the pickle is barely warm. When reusing jars cover with a square of plastic wrap before putting on the lid. If you are using multiple small jars, perhaps for gifts, be sure to evenly distribute the peppers, chile, and oil in each.

Mature for 10 days before eating. It will keep for months in the refrigerator.

Sweet Mango Chutney

Type: Indian
Speed: Over an hour
Notes: Sweet mango chutney is certainly the most popular of Indian condiments in the West. I like it particularly with Besan Pancakes (page 59) or Chana Masala (page 98).

- 5 firm, barely ripe mangos, peeled and chopped (about 2 ½ pounds)
- 1 ounce ginger, peeled and minced
- 1 bulb garlic, peeled and minced (about 12 cloves)

- 1 cup white wine vinegar
- ¼ teaspoon salt
- ½ to 1 teaspoon cayenne pepper
- 2 cups brown sugar
- ¼ teaspoon ground cloves

Prepare the ginger and garlic and blend in a food processor with the vinegar. Once you have a paste, tip the contents into a large saucepan with all the other ingredients. Bring the pan to a boil, then simmer on low heat for an hour. Stir to prevent burning toward the end of cooking. Prepare sterilized jars with boiling water, making sure they are completely dry. Spoon in the chutney, leave the lid slightly ajar until it has cooled a little, then seal and refrigerate.

Tamarind Dipping Sauce

Type: Indian
Speed: Fast
Notes: This dipping sauce for Samosas (page 39) and Pakoras (page 232) should be thick enough to coat the surface of the snack, but not as thick as honey. This is quite spicy, so halve the cayenne for a milder version.

- 2 tablespoons tamarind concentrate
- ½ cup hot water
- ½ cup brown sugar
- 1 tablespoon cayenne pepper
- 1 teaspoon ginger powder

- 1 tablespoon mango powder
- ½ teaspoon garam masala
- 1 tablespoon cumin powder
- 1 teaspoon salt
- ½ teaspoon roasted besan (chickpea flour)

In a saucepan, dissolve the tamarind in the water, then add the brown sugar. Mix all the rest of the ingredients in a small bowl making sure there are no lumps. Bring the saucepan to a boil, then add the spice mixture. Simmer uncovered and reduce to the desired thickness. Refrigerate the sauce until needed.

Tomato Chutney

Type: South Indian
Speed: Less than an hour
Notes: This acidic sweet chutney goes well with creamy, rich dishes like Jackfruit in Coconut-Cashew Sauce (page 106) or Cashew Soup (page 47).

Pickles & Chutneys

- 8 ounces sugar
- ½ cup water
- ½ cup white wine vinegar
- 2 cloves garlic, sliced
- 4 bay leaves
- 1 teaspoon cayenne pepper

- ¼ teaspoon garam masala
- 1½ teaspoon black onion (nigella) seeds
- 1 pound tomatoes, coarsely chopped

Bring the sugar, water, and vinegar to a boil in a small saucepan. Add the rest of the ingredients and return to a boil. Reduce the heat to low and simmer uncovered until the chutney thickens, about 35 minutes. Place into a sterilized jar. Refrigerate after opening.

Currant Taste

As I mentioned, I grew up quite uninterested in candy and, to a degree, desserts. One exception was the school lunch, which on occasion included something we called a wagon wheel with pink custard. They were hard, flat cookies, half vanilla and half chocolate flavored. That was a treat because some of the menu alternatives could be grim indeed. A dessert I didn't warm to was a kind of cake with currants. I remember my brother telling me that currants were dead flies; that was the end of any interest in a whole genre of desserts, which mostly continues to this day. I'm no longer sure if that association, even though I never really believed it was true, squashed my desire or if I just don't usually care for embedded currants in cake or other desserts.

Desserts

A rich dessert is the Holy Grail for vegans. Without dairy, the satisfying fats can make ice cream or pudding taste bland and even watery. I have rarely found a vegan ice cream or chocolate pudding that passes the taste test. With a few exceptions, they just satisfy that after-dinner sweet craving, but sometimes the aftertaste can be pasty. Again, my philosophy is not to imitate dairy dishes. Instead, I have concentrated on desserts that are either traditionally dairy-free or that need minimum tweaking. Although some of these traditional desserts are sweet and flavorful, they are not a replacement for desserts like ice cream. I remain unconvinced in that department. If the selection here seems a little too biased toward the rich and heavy, it's because those textures are perhaps less available to vegans, and I take it as given that most people can prepare a light fruit salad or snack on dried figs.

My favorite approach for dessert is the variety tray. This works for both Arabian and Indian meals and allows for some artistic flair to boot.

Carrot Dessert

Type: Indian
Preparation: You will need Almond Syrup (page 18)
Speed: Less than an hour
Notes: Indian sweets and desserts are usually very sweet. This colorful dessert is no exception. It is rich and a small amount goes a long way. This should be enough for 4 or 5 people.

- 1 pound carrots, grated
- 3 tablespoons coconut oil
- 1 cup Almond Syrup (page 18)
- Juice from ½ a small lemon
- A few broken almonds for garnish

Heat oil in a saucepan. Add carrots and fry for 10 minutes. Add the almond syrup. Simmer for another 20 minutes. Stir in the lemon juice, heat through, and serve hot in bowls garnished with broken almonds and perhaps a few raspberries. It can also be eaten cold.

Desserts

Coconut Berry Surprise

Type: Indian
Speed: Less than an hour
Notes: An Indian dessert tray should present a variety of temptations. Here fresh berries and hidden inside sweetened coconut balls. For fussy or less adventurous guests, you can flag the berry by adding a flash of color to the top. Refrigerate them until ready to serve.

- ⅓ cup coconut oil
- 2 cups desiccated coconut
- 3 tablespoons sugar
- ½ cup coconut cream

- A few fresh blueberries
- A few fresh raspberries
- A few small fresh alpine strawberries

Stir the coconut oil, coconut and sugar in a saucepan over low heat for a few minutes. The mixture should start to appear sticky. Add the coconut cream and continue stirring for 2 or 3 minutes until it is cooked through.

Let the mixture stand for a few minutes until it is cool enough to handle.

Take a portion of the mixture about the size of walnut in its shell. Insert a berry into the center and form a ball around it. If you want to flag the different berries, keep each flavor separate. Place them on a plate, cover with plastic wrap, and refrigerate until needed.

To flag the berries you can paint a small color flash on the balls using different colored food coloring.

Desserts

Coconut Halva

Type: Indian
Speed: About 30 minutes
Notes: The texture of this Indian sweet is quite buttery and is normally made with ghee. Halva is a mud brown color, so if you can find pure silver or gold foil, it makes a very nice garnish. A dusting of powdered sugar will work too.

- ½ cup sugar
- ½ cup water
- ½ cup coconut oil
- ½ cup besan (chickpea flour)
- 2 tablespoons coconut cream

- ½ teaspoon rose water
- ½ cup mixed blanched almond slivers, diced dried apricots, diced dried dates, and golden raisins
- 1 cup almond meal

Boil the sugar and water to make a syrup and set aside.

Heat the coconut oil in a skillet and sieve in the besan while constantly stirring. Cook the besan on medium-low heat until it turns a shade darker, about a minute. Turn off the heat and let it cool for 10 minutes, then stir in the syrup, nuts and dried fruits, coconut cream, and rose water.

Now bring the heat back on to medium and stir constantly until the mixture thickens. This will be about 5 minutes and the mixture will darken a little more. The mixture should now be quite stiff. Remove the pan from the heat and fold in the almond meal.

Tip the mixture into a greased tray and refrigerate until it is fully set. I like to cut this buttery version into triangles. Sometimes a little excess oil will solidify around the edge of the tray. This can be simply trimmed off with a sharp knife. You can make halva ahead of time. It's nice to present a mixture of small desserts with a buffet-style or *thali* Indian meal.

Desserts

Date Royal

Type: Arabian
Speed: About 30 minutes
Notes: A sweet plate is a useful addition to a buffet-style meal. As people sit and talk, they can finish with Sesame Candy (page 183) or these stuffed dates.

- Dates
- Walnuts for stuffing
- ½ cup tahini
- ¼ cup blue agave syrup

- 1 teaspoon anise seeds
- ½ cup hazelnuts
- Anise seeds for garnish

Slit the dates lengthwise and remove the stone. I like to use medjool or my favorite jet-black abbada dates, but either way the more malleable varieties work the best. With half of the dates, replace the stone with half a walnut and squeeze it back into shape, leaving a little nut poking out for identification. The other half can be filled with this sweet halva filling.

Put the tahini, syrup, and anise seeds in a strong food processor (this paste gets quite stiff). Process until the paste is mixed and smooth. Add the hazelnuts and process until they are small chunks. Using a teaspoon fill each of the remaining dates and close leaving a small strip of paste exposed on top. Place anise seeds on a plate and dip the top of each date in so that the anise sticks to it. Serve by alternating the halva dates with the walnut dates around a decorative plate with perhaps a pile of almonds, dried apricots, or sesame candy in the center.

Desserts

Deep-Fried Batter (Jalebi) in Kewra Syrup

Type: Indian
Preparation: You will have an hour while the batter sits
Speed: Fast
Notes: This traditional dessert is made in the shape of a pretzel by circling a dispenser above hot oil while squeezing in the batter. This dessert, as is often the case in India, is very sweet.

- 1 teaspoon sugar
- 1 teaspoon active yeast
- 1 tablespoon warm water
- 1 cup all-purpose flour

- 2 tablespoons besan (chickpea flour)
- 1 teaspoon light oil (such as canola)
- Pinch of salt
- 1 cup warm water

For the syrup:

- 1 cup sugar
- ½ cup water
- 1 tablespoon lemon juice

- 1 tablespoon kewra water
- Zest from 1 lemon

Oil for deep frying

In a bowl, mix the sugar and yeast with a tablespoon of warm water. Let it sit for 2 minutes and then stir in the flour, besan, oil, salt, and the cup of warm water. Stir to eliminate any lumps, then set aside and prepare the syrup. In a saucepan, bring the water, sugar, and lemon juice to a boil. Reduce the heat to low and stir in the kewra water. If kewra water is unavailable you can try other flavors such as rose water, orange flower water, or almond extract. Simmer for a few minutes while stirring, and then remove the pan from the heat. The batter needs to sour for an hour in a warmish spot before filling the mustard bottle (of course it must be thoroughly cleaned first).

Fill a deep frying pan to the depth of an inch and heat until a drop of batter sizzles when dropped in. Try to keep the heat evenly on medium. Circle the bottle above the oil squeezing evenly. As the batter drags against the oil, you can form a pretzel shape and with practice you can form quite neat uniform shapes. After a few second you can flip each jalebi over and fry the other side. Lay the jalebis out on a paper towel. They should be golden brown. Now reheat the syrup and dunk each jalebi for a few seconds and lay out on a platter. Once they are arranged on a platter, spoon a little remaining syrup over and them and garnish with lemon zest.

Desserts

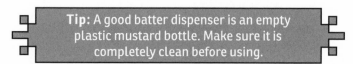

Tip: A good batter dispenser is an empty plastic mustard bottle. Make sure it is completely clean before using.

Donuts in Syrup

Type: Lebanese
Preparation: You will need Orange Flower Syrup (page 23). You will have a few hours while the batter rises.
Speed: Less than an hour
Notes: Serve this very sweet dessert in a shallow dish after a Lebanese meal.

- ¼-ounce packet of yeast, dissolved in 2 tablespoons warm water
- 3 cups all-purpose flour
- 1 teaspoon salt
- 2 tablespoons cornstarch
- 2 cups warm water
- Oil for deep frying
- 1 cup Orange Flower Syrup (page 23)

Dissolve the yeast in water and let it stand for 10 minutes. Mix the flour, salt, cornstarch, and dissolved yeast together in a large bowl. Add the warm water and beat with a fork until all of the lumps have been absorbed. The mixture should be about the consistency of a thick batter. Cover it with plastic wrap and set aside in a warm area for at least 2 hours.

Heat the oil in a skillet (enough to fill to a depth of about 3 inches) on medium-high heat. Place a tray, or large plate, covered with a paper towels next to the stove along with a small bowl of water, a couple more paper towels, and the donut batter. Using a small wet spoon, scoop up a spoonful of batter. Use your finger to fold over any hanging batter. Carefully slide the batter into the oil. It should immediately cause the batter to puff up. Repeat while there is room in the skillet, keeping the spoon clean and wet between each. With a fork, roll the donuts to ensure an even fry. When each donut is golden, remove with a slotted spoon and move onto the paper towel–covered plate. Repeat until the batter is gone.

In a shallow bowl, arrange the donuts discarding the paper towel. Pour over the thick honey like Orange Flower Syrup or thin a portion by warming it in a small saucepan with a little water. Serve warm or cold.

Durian Dessert

Type: Asian
Speed: Very fast
Notes: Deservedly known as the king of all fruit. Even though this fruit is not traditional to the cuisines dealt with in this book, I wanted to include a recipe for durian. The problem is that durian is so rich, creamy, and flavorful that almost anything you add is redundant. In Malaysia there are a number of durian-flavored foods such as ice cream, chocolate-covered durian, etc. But sometimes only the untainted experience will do. The divide between those who do and don't like the fruit seems absolute. For those like me who adore it, no explanation is necessary. For the rest it's usually the overpowering smell or lingering flavor that is the deal-breaker. Sometimes even the very look of the flesh is off-putting.

You will need at least 6 fragrant pears for a smallish durian. The crispness and flavor of this variety of pear is important and I really recommend you seek them out. A very crisp Asian pear apple might be an acceptable substitute.

- 1 small durian
- Several fragrant pears

- Juice from ½ a lemon

Remove the cream-colored sacks of flesh from the durian making sure every cavity is evacuated. Remove the large brown seeds and immediately dispose of them and the spiky shell outside in the compost to reduce the smell.

Place the flesh in a food processor and process to a custard-like consistency. Mix the lemon juice with a couple of cups of water in a bowl.

Cut a flat segment off the top of a pear, removing the stalk and enabling it to stand upright. Do the same at the other end, then cut the pear in the same direction to make two egg cup–like halves. Carefully remove the cores leaving a cavity. Place the halves in the lemon water and repeat until all the pears are made into cups. The amount of pears needed depends on the size of the durian and how many guests are present.

Once all of the pears are prepared, dry them with a paper towel and arrange them on a decorative plate. Fill each one with a generous dollop of durian so it forms a nice dome above each half pear. You can garnish each with a little cocoa powder or fine mint strips for plate design.

Desserts

Halva

Type: Arabian
Speed: Fast
Notes: Halva is very sweet and filling. It's best to make the serving portions quite small.

- ⅓ cup water
- 1 cup sugar
- Juice from 1 small lemon
- 1 cup tahini

- 1 tablespoon vanilla extract
- 2 tablespoons unsalted shelled pistachios (or slivered almonds)

Bring the water, sugar, and lemon juice to a boil, then reduce the heat and simmer for 2 minutes. Set aside. Heat the tahini over medium heat in a saucepan until bubbles start to form around the edge. Keep heating and stir for a few minutes. It will start to harden up in patches. Transfer the tahini to the syrup and add the vanilla and pistachios, then stir to a smooth paste. Line a baking tray with greaseproof paper and pour in the mixture.

Refrigerate the halva for at least 24 hours before cutting into triangles or squares and serving.

Kumquat Coffee Dessert

Type: North African/Sicilian
Preparation: You will need Almond Syrup (page 23)
Speed: Less than half an hour
Notes: This bittersweet dessert is adapted from methods used in the Mediterranean, particularly in Sicily.

- 2½ cups water
- ½ cup sugar
- 30 kumquats
- 1 tablespoon cocoa powder

- 2 tablespoons instant coffee
- ½ cup Almond Syrup (page 23)
- ⅓ cup cornstarch
- A little more water

Bring the water to a boil in a saucepan, add sugar, and dissolve. Trim the stalks off the kumquats, cut them in half, and deseed. Add them to the pot and boil for 5 minutes. Remove the kumquats and set aside. Stir in the cocoa powder, instant coffee, and almond syrup. Mix the cornstarch with enough water to make slurry, about ½ cup altogether. As the pan boils add the cornstarch solution, constantly stirring for about 30 seconds, making sure that there are no lumps. Place into dessert dishes. Use the boiled kumquats to decorate each dessert, then refrigerate for an hour.

Desserts

Lime-Mint-Guava Dessert

Type: Sicilian
Speed: Fast
Notes: This is an otherworldly-looking dessert adapted from a traditional Sicilian preparation. Like Jell-O, it's just a flavor-delivery medium and you could experiment with various flavor extracts. It may also go down well with kids. This version is a milky translucent jell with a light green hue. The lime peel should be left in long strands. It looks very nice suspended in the dessert.

- 2 cups water
- 1 large bunch fresh spearmint
- 1 lime
- ⅔ cup sugar
- ¼ cup cornstarch
- A little more water
- About 8 fresh guava or feijoa (pineapple guava)

Bring the water to a boil in a saucepan, add the mint leaves, and turn off the heat. Reserve a few crowns of mint for garnish. Let the mint steep for 5 minutes. Meanwhile, carefully zest the green peel from the lime, trying not to remove too much white pith. Set it aside.

Using a spoon, squeeze the mint against the side of the saucepan to extract as much flavor as possible. Strain the liquid into a new pan and discard the mint.

Squeeze the juice from the lime into the new pan, then add the sugar and peel. Bring the mixture to a boil on a medium heat for a couple of minutes. Put the corn flour in a measuring container and add enough water to form a slurry of about ⅓ of a cup. Skin and coarsely chop the guava and divide them between glass dessert dishes.

Add the cornstarch slurry to the saucepan and stir for about 30 seconds, then pour into the dishes. Refrigerate the desserts for a few hours. Garnish with the top crown of a sprig of mint.

Desserts

Nut Brittle

Type: Arabian
Speed: Very fast
Notes: Although the brittle is almost 100 percent sugar, once melted it takes on a bittersweet taste.

- 1 cup sugar
- ½ cup raw almonds
- ½ cup shelled unsalted pistachio nuts

Line a small baking tray with greaseproof paper. Arrange the nuts evenly across the bottom, almost touching, in a single layer.

In a small saucepan, melt the sugar over medium heat constantly stirring. As it turns liquid, it will slowly darken to a rich amber color. As soon as all of the sugar is liquid, pour it over the nuts to cover. Let cool. After a couple of minutes you can score the brittle to encourage it to break in squares once fully hardened, or skip that stage and place in the freezer until needed and simply break it into pieces.

> **Tip:** Nut brittle quickly becomes sticky from the heat of your fingers alone. Try folding mint leaves around the bottom of each piece to act as a holder. This will also make an attractive display when arranged on a plate.

Desserts

Orange Sesame Candy

Type: Arabian
Speed: Less than an hour
Notes: This traditional candy is very sweet but usually made with honey. There are many variations: some with nuts, some with flavoring. My version has orange zest to add bitterness against a mix of syrups and sugars.

- ⅓ cup agave syrup
- 2 tablespoons sugar
- 1 tablespoon maple syrup
- 1 tablespoon dehydrated cane juice
- 1 cup sesame seeds
- Zest from 2 medium oranges
- Small pinch of salt
- 1 teaspoon orange blossom water

Mix the agave, sugar, maple syrup, and dehydrated cane juice in a saucepan. Bring to a boil, then reduce the heat to a low simmer.

Dry roast the sesame seeds until they start to smell toasted and turn a slight shade darker. Add to the saucepan and mix. Simmer for about 7 or 8 minutes. The mix should start to get a golden, glazed look. Fold in the orange zest, salt, and orange blossom water. Keep stirring the mixture and simmer for about 4 minutes. It is important at this stage that the mixture has reduced sufficiently or it will not set. Do not reduce the mixture too much or the candy may become brittle like glass.

Once ready, let the mixture cool just a little and pour onto a greaseproof paper, scraping it all into a pile. Flatten roughly with the side of a knife and herd it into a rough, flat square. Cover with another sheet of greaseproof paper and roll flat with a rolling pin to remove any air pockets. The candy dries quickly, so while it's still warm score it with a sharp knife into strips. You may need to keep the knife from accumulating matter by dipping it in hot water. Cut the strips into 2-inch sections, then mold into individual candy logs with your hands. Store in the refrigerator.

Desserts

Orange Slices in Syrup

Type: North African
Preparation: You will need Orange Flower Syrup (page 23)
Speed: Fast
Notes: A bright addition to the table.

- 2 oranges
- 3 tablespoons unsalted pistachios, shelled
- About ½ cup Orange Flower Syrup (page 23)

Zest the orange peel into thin slivers using a citrus zester or grater. Blanch in boiling water, pat dry, and set aside.

Peel the oranges and divide into segments. Remove any seeds. Using a sharp knife, trim away the pith.

Arrange the segments in a shallow bowl and ladle the syrup over them. Note that although the syrup is quite thick the orange slices will release some juice and thin it somewhat. Garnish with the orange zest and pistachios. Serve cold.

White Mulberry Dessert

Type: Arabian
Speed: Very quick
Notes: White mulberries are not always easy to find in the West. In Turkey they grow abundantly and are easily available dried across the region. This is a dessert adaptation of a breakfast dish. Mulberries are very sweet, so serve in small portions.

- 1 cup dried white mulberries
- 1 cup almond milk
- 1 tablespoon slivered almonds for garnish

Desserts

Simply blend the mulberries and almond milk in a food processor until you have a relatively smooth porridge consistency. You could add blueberries for color or a tart barberry if you wish. Turn into small bowls and then garnish with the slivered almonds. Eat cold.

Jersey Krishna

In the '80s I lived in New York City for about 7 years, and for one special occasion, some friends asked me along to an "Indian" vegetarian restaurant. It was one of those places dedicated to a guru of some hue. The staff, far from being Indian, were nevertheless members of a Hindu sect and quietly shuffled around in understated robes. In the storefront was a glass enclosure with a throne for the head holy man should he drop by. At this time in New York the Hari Krishna movement had again become popular and had even infiltrated the hardcore punk scene (Krishnacore).

The food was laid out buffet-style on a long wooden table in three distinct categories. The first was hippy-type grains and salads in large bowls. In the center was typical NYC Italian fare: spaghetti, lasagna, pizza, etc. Lastly came a number of bowls of highly Americanized Indian food: rice pilaf, tofu in gravy . . .

My jaw dropped as I saw the hefty locals pile their plates with food from all three areas, albeit light on the first, sit down, and tuck in. Lasagna and curry, really!

Sample Menus

It has occurred to me that, like many English, some Americans hold a tenuous grasp of the concept of a cuisine. Times have changed and more recently with the popularity of Japanese, Thai, Ethiopian, and Mexican restaurants, people follow their fancy and do manage to experience the complementary flavors a cuisine offers. That, however, is eating out. What about at home?

When one looks at the diet in the West it is appalling to discover just how few types of food are embraced and the shoddy fashion in which it is eaten. In fact, most people seem to rotate less than half a dozen items: pizza, burger, pasta, fries, etc. eaten on the couch in front of the TV. Food on the run is of course a necessity at times, but not ideal. I wonder if, compared to a well-organized kitchen, fast food really is faster. I'm not sure.

I was never a fan of the potluck concept for the above reasons. I suppose it can work in the right setting but I'm way too fastidious when it comes to a sit-down setting. When laying out a southern Indian meal, for example, the bowl of pasta salad is an annoying blemish. I love the concept of a carefully planed meal, the aesthetics being as crucial as the smell and taste. It doesn't have to be fancy; a light summer lunch can be just a chilled drink and a small Moroccan salad with olives, but when it is presented well, it's usually memorable.

Sometimes bewildered omnivores ask me what I eat. If I care to answer such a leading question, I list some fruits that I have eaten in the past month: cherimoya, sapote, durian, mangosteen, rambutan, jackfruit, star fruit—most of which they haven't even heard of, let alone eaten. I then reply, "and you?" That's the supercilious answer this tiresome, ill-informed question deserves. Still, in this regard I don't like to repeat the same dish too soon. Instead, leftovers from a main course would be frozen and reappear a week or two later as a side dish.

Indian (Clockwise from top left)

- Bitter Melons and Onion (page 60)
- Tomato Chutney (page 168)
- Chile Citrus Pickle (page 151)

Northern Indian #1 (Clockwise from top left)

- Basmati Northern Style (page 126)
- Chapati (page 32)
- Moong Dal with Garlic (page 67)
- Almond Drink (page 209)
- Fruit and Nut Chutney (page 154)
- Lemon Peel and Onion Relish (page 227)
- Coconut Halva (page 175)
- Potatoes and Cauliflower in Gravy (page 118)
- Baingan Bharta (page 94)

Indian
- Cashew Soup (page 47)

Moroccan (Clockwise from top left)
- Black Vegetable Medley (page 223)
- Butternut Squash Soup (page 46)
- Moroccan Bread (page 34)
- Moroccan Orange and Black Olive Salad (page 141)
- Mint Tea (page 212)

North Indian (Clockwise from top left)

- Vegetable Samosas (page 39)
- Tamarind Sauce (page 168)
- Lime Pickle (page 158)
- Fruit and Nut Chutney (page 154)

Lebanese (Clockwise from top left)

- Humus (page 70)
- Pita Bread (page 35)
- Ajvar (page 137)
- Spinach Pie (page 37)
- Orange Sesame Candy (page 183)
- Baba Ghanoush (page 58)
- Spicy Fava Bean Salad (page 145)

Southern Indian (Clockwise from top left)

- Sambar (page 78)
- Mango Rice (page 129)
- Longan and Onion Chutney (page 159)
- Jackfruit in Coconut-Cashew Sauce (page 106)
- Lime Pickle (page 158)
- Coconut Chutney (page 152)
- Pineapple and Date Chutney (page 164)
- Peanut Vada (page 74)

North African #1 (Clockwise from top left)

- Moroccan Bread (page 34)
- Moroccan Orange and Black Olive Salad (page 141)
- Mint Tea (page 212)
- Black Vegetable Medley (page 223)

- Harissa/Za'atar Dip (page 155 and page 146)
- Preserved Lemons (page 165)
- Date Royal (page 176)
- Butternut Squash Soup (page 46)

Lebanese (Clockwise from top left)
- Pita Bread (page 35)
- Spinach Pie (page 37)
- Ajvar (page 137)

Northern Indian #2 (Clockwise from top left)

- Okra North Indian Style (page 115)
- Mint Chutney (page 161)
- Sweet Mango Chutney (page 167)
- Savory Brussels Sprouts (page 79)
- Flax Roti (page 33)
- Fenugreek Purée (page 66)
- Nut Brittle (page 182)
- Mango Lassi (page 211)
- Lime Rice Pilaf (page 128)
- Besan Pancakes (page 59)

North Indian (From the left)

- Flax Roti (page 33)
- Nut Brittle (page 182)
- Savory Brussels Sprouts (page 79)

Indian #1 (Clockwise from top left)

- Poori (page 36)
- Cauliflower, Potato, and Methi Curry (page 97)
- Bitter Melons and Onion (page 60)
- Tomato Chutney (page 168)
- Chile Citrus Pickle (page 151)
- Coconut Berry Surprise (page 174)
- Cashew Soup (page 47)

Egyptian (Clockwise from top left)

- Lime-Mint-Guava Dessert (page 181)
- Fūl Mudammas (page 104)
- Bread Topped with Za'atar (page 31)
- Cucumber Salad (page 139)

Indian

- Lime Rice Pilaf (page 128)

• Hummus (page 70)

• Black Vegetable Medley (page 223)

North African #2 (Clockwise from top left)

- Pita Bread (page 35)
- Angelica Tea (page 209)
- Halva (page 180)
- Eggplant and Chickpeas (page 100)

North Indian

Indian
- Coconut Halva (page 175)

Lebanese (Left to right)
- Ajvar (page 137)
- Spicy Fava Bean Salad (page 145)

Indian (Clockwise from top left)

- Moong Dal (page 67)
- Fruit and Nut Chutney (page 154)
- Lemon Peel and Onion Relish (page 227)
- Chapati (page 32)

Sex, Veggies, and Rock 'n' Roll

The reunion tour in '97 was my first full U.S. tour by road. With special guests Anti-Flag, we spent 6 weeks circling the country in a huge airport shuttle bus I bought from Samiam. It was equipped with electric doors, intercom, TV, and video. At the back was a security cage for the gear and in the main cabin were bunk beds. It was an arduous tour for sure, but one advantage was that I could bring food with me and was quite content to sit outside in the parking lot while the rest were in the steakhouse or sushi restaurant. Furthermore, by way of insurance, I traveled with a juicer. I think word got around, and from time to time fans would show up with bags of carrots for me. Rock 'n' roll!

Drinks

For many these days, beer seems to be the drink of choice to accompany Indian food. I'm not a drinker, so I can't really comment about that particular combination. Despite myriad religious conventions, alcohol, particularly liquors, has always been available in India but exotic and interesting nonalcoholic beverages naturally prevail.

Ever resourceful, Indians can seem to make use of every plant around for food, drink, dyes, hair products, and so on. Even something as unlikely as besan (chickpea flour) is transformed into a malty drink (page 210) at the hands of the Indians. What are not covered in this book are the yogurt and dairy drinks like lassi (except my fake mango lassi) and milky chai. For my taste, a straw in a drinking coconut, chilled watermelon (page 213), sugar cane juice, or lime-flavored water are perfect to accompany a robust Indian meal. Perhaps for a lighter Indian snack, a glass of fruit punch would go well.

Across India, and many other regions, coconut water is drunk directly from the green drinking coconut. It is very refreshing on hot summers day but is not to be confused with coconut milk, which is made by boiling the white flesh and then straining the liquid. These days, drinking coconuts are widely available from Thai, Chinese, or Indian stores usually stripped of the green skin. Coconut water seems to have become a popular sports drink and is now available in cartons. There's no better drink to accompany southern Indian food than coconut water drunk directly from the shell. I bought a coconut tool in Brazil, which bores a hole through the shell, but a sharp, clean screwdriver can be hammered through one of the eyes. Insert a straw, or better still an Angelica straw, and you're good to go.

In the Arab world, alcohol is often prohibited. Don't be taken in—in Morocco "Berber whisky" is the nickname for Mint Tea (page 212). In the modern era soda bottles and cans are everywhere in these countries. In Karachi the piles of strewn plastic bottles and trash reach knee high in some areas. I've witnessed people simply putting a match to it. On the other hand, I have never seen a can of soda as cheap as in Syria when I was there a few years ago, but the empty cans and bottles are well guarded, as the loss of them can be the loss of any profit. For the tourist, canned drinks, particularly in India and Pakistan, are not a bad idea to try and dodge the "Delhi belly."

Tea, of course, is very popular and so are flavored syrup drinks such as Almond Syrup (page 209). Although very sweet and perhaps not the best choice for regular consumption, these syrups diluted and poured over ice are fantastic on a hot summer day.

Almond Drink

Type: Indian
Preparation: You will need Almond Syrup (page 18)
Speed: Very fast
Notes: Over ice, this almond drink is a real summer refresher. I'm sure it would also work with an alcohol booster, as it is quite rich. It's best to fill the glass with ice cubes or the drink will be overpoweringly sweet.

- 1 part Almond Syrup (page 18) to 2 parts water
- Ice cubes
- A few sprigs of mint for garnish

Thoroughly mix the syrup and water in a pitcher. Pour into long glasses filled with ice cubes. Garnish with a sprig of mint.

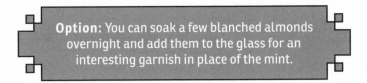

Option: You can soak a few blanched almonds overnight and add them to the glass for an interesting garnish in place of the mint.

Angelica Tea

Type: Arabian
Speed: Fast
Notes: Angelica is best known as an addition to cakes when the stem is crystallized but the root and seeds are also used to flavor gin. In some parts of the world the root is eaten and the hollow stems are even made into musical wind instruments. This is enough for a small gathering, served in Arabian tea glasses.

- 2 ounces angelica leaves
- ½ teaspoon green tea
- 3½ cups water
- Sugar

Bring the water to a boil. Warm a teapot using half a cup of the hot water, throw the water out, and put in the angelica leaves and green tea. Pour on the remaining hot water and leave to steep for 5 minutes. Serve strained into small tea glasses with a bowl of sugar to add to each glass according to taste.

Drinks

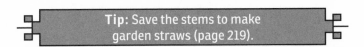

Tip: Save the stems to make garden straws (page 219).

Ayran

Type: Arabian
Speed: Fast
Notes: My variation on mint ayran.

- 2½ cups water
- 1 large bunch of fresh mint
- ½ teaspoon salt

- 2 cups unsweetened, plain soy yogurt
- A few crushed ice cubes

Bring the water to boil in a small pan. Reduce the heat to a simmer, add the fresh washed mint, and stir to submerge. Reserve a few pristine leaves for garnish. Turn off the heat and let the mint steep for 10 minutes. Press the mint against the side of the pan with the back of a spoon to release as much flavor as possible, then strain the mint water into a plastic container, add the salt and place it in the freezer until it's cold. In a large Tupperware container or a blender, mix the mint water, yogurt, and ice. Shake or blend it until frothy. Serve in long glasses garnished with mint leaves.

Chickpea Flour Drink

Type: North Indian
Speed: Fast
Notes: In the UK, many people enjoy malt milk drinks like Horlicks or Ovaltine, particularly before bedtime. This drink has a similar type of flavor but is a vegan version from North India. It is easy and quick to make.

- 1 tablespoon coconut oil
- 2 tablespoons besan (chickpea flour)
- Seeds from 2 cardamom pods, crushed

- 2 cups water
- 2 tablespoons sugar

Heat the oil in a saucepan. Once hot, add the besan and ground cardamom seeds. Keep scraping the flour from the pan surface and stirring until it turns a light caramel color. Do not burn. Add the water, bring to a boil, and then dissolve the sugar in. Stir and simmer for couple of minutes. Serve hot in teacups or mugs.

Drinks

Hibiscus Flower Tea

Type: Arabian
Speed: Fast
Notes: Hibiscus drink is sold in some health food stores. The flower imparts a nice red color to this refreshing tea.

- 2 cups water
- 6 dried hibiscus flowers
- 2 ginger, peeled and sliced
- 1 tablespoon sugar
- 4 whole cloves

Bring the water to boil in a small pan. Reduce the heat to a simmer and add all of the ingredients. Simmer for 5 minutes and then strain. Drink hot or chill in the refrigerator.

Mango Lassi

Type: Indian
Preparation: You will need a cup of Almond Syrup (page 18)
Speed: Fast
Notes: This thick mango drink is not strictly a lassi because it is dairy-free. I like to use the bright yellow manila (Ataulfo) mangos not only for their sweet flavor, but because they are generally fiber-free.

- ½ pound chopped mango
- 1 cup Almond Syrup (page 18)
- ½ cup water
- 2 ounces fresh pineapple
- Ice cubes

Blend all the ingredients, except the ice, in a blender until smooth. Serve in long glasses over ice cubes.

Drinks

Mint Tea

Type: Moroccan
Speed: Fast
Notes: Mint tea, or "Berber whisky" as it is sometimes known, is taken many times a day in Morocco. It is traditionally made very sweet and is always generously loaded with fresh mint. I have left the amounts open, dependent on how many people are taking tea, but make sure there is sufficient mint—a good-sized bunch for a couple of cups. The small glass teacups normally have a teaspoon of sugar, but that might be a little sweet for some.

- 1 large bunch of fresh spearmint
- Water
- Pinch of green tea
- Sugar

Bring the water to boil in a small kettle or pan. Preheat a teapot with a little boiling water. Discard that water, fill the pot with fresh mint, add boiling water to cover the mint, and then add the green tea. Let the tea steep for a few minutes before pouring into small tea glasses or teacups through a strainer. Add sugar to taste.

> **Option:** For tourists, the locals serve the tea in a glass with the leaves still in. Better is to simply garnish with a fresh sprig of mint.

Drinks

Quince Quencher

Type: Arabian
Speed: 15 minutes
Notes: This very sweet drink should be served in long glasses over ice.

- 3½ cups water
- 1½ cups sugar
- ½ cup lemon juice

- 2 large quinces, juiced
- 6 more cups water
- A few mint leaves for garnish

Bring the water to boil in a large saucepan. Fully dissolve the sugar in the pan. Meanwhile, juice the quinces using a juicer. Add the lemon and quince juice to the saucepan and reduce the heat to a low simmer for 5 minutes. Pour into a large pitcher and add 6 more cups of water. Set aside to cool, then refrigerate covered with plastic wrap.

If you serve this over crushed ice it may dilute the drink somewhat, but this recipe is on the strong side.

When ready to serve pour into tall glasses full of ice cubes (or crushed ice) and top off with a couple of mint leaves.

Watermelon-Basil Juice

Type: Arabian
Speed: Very fast
Notes: This drink is sweet without the addition of any sugar.

- One chilled watermelon

- 1 bunch of basil

Wash the basil and run it through the juicer. Cut the red flesh off the watermelon into strips and run through the juicer. Reserve small triangles of melon (leave a strip of skin on top) to garnish the top of each glass. Stir and serve in long glasses.

> **Option:** With a sharp knife, carefully cut away the white portion of the rind close to the green peel. Grate the rind into a bowl and save for Watermelon Rind Bharta (page 237).

Drinks

On a Budget

In the mid-'70s I found myself in Colliers Wood in south London. For many of us the great hope of the new punk movement was to embrace its freedoms by removing ourselves from society's conventions and restraints. We didn't want jobs or London's crippling rent, so squatting became the order of the day. I was held up in a two-bedroom house on an un-noteworthy residential street, along with an out-of-work Irish laborer, and a couple of older guys who can best be described as survivors of a Mad Max–type apocalypse. On the surface it wasn't ideal, but miraculously nothing untoward transpired, at least not involving me. As the other occupants peeled away, one to Brixton prison, the others to destinations unknown, I was left to work out the logistics of surviving on next to no money. At this time, I was rehearsing in a punk band before the UK Subs that was always looking for a drummer. We were called the Specimens. I did some work for a temp agency, which allowed me to legitimately maintain utilities and left some money for provisions. At some point funds stretched to facilitate the purchase of a 56-pound sack of potatoes and a smaller sack of onions. This became my staple for the next few months. French fries, or chips as we call them, mashed potatoes, baked potatoes, onion rings, fried onions, onion soup, onion and potato soup, potato soup . . . the options were rigorously explored. To supplement this scant base I would buy day-old bread from the supermarket and gather various edibles from Wimbledon common. It seemed that I could actually sustain myself on pennies a day, albeit for a finite period.

Almost two decades later in San Francisco, again rehearsing with a band—this time Ten Bright Spikes—I repeated the experiment over one summer. (Thankfully the second time around was not from necessity.) This time I used only the supplies already stocked in my cupboards and supplemented with fresh supplies from Golden Gate Park, two blocks south of our house in the Richmond district. My filling for the Date Royal (page 176) recipe comes from this time. The last of my lavish resources were gathered for one last indulgence, thus the designation "Royal." After rationing out supplies this makeshift candy was anticipated like a banquette fit for the monarchy. In fact all flavors started to be magnified and one choose each ingredient with great care and relished the results. What I took from both of these experiences is the idea of supplementing inexpensive provisions, such as dried beans or rice, with free or recycled ingredients to create a nutritious meal on a budget.

Recycled

I find it amazing that people in the West will pay $3.99 or more for a tiny tray of blackberries, when they are up for grabs growing free all around the city and in the park. When they come into season, I gather blackberries up in Marin County and freeze them for later use. It takes only a few minutes to pick more than a pound. Stinging nettles are another plant ignored in favor of expensive commercially grown greens like spinach. If you can navigate the stings, it is a great, easy-to-find culinary plant.

I also pick the wild nasturtium seeds to pickle (page 229). They grow all over Northern California. Additionally, a few edible nasturtium flowers are also useful to add a colorful element to salads or as a garnish. This is also an excellent venture for children to teach them a little about where food comes from and give them a break from the computer screen.

Growing your own food is so satisfying. It's puzzling that most people don't bother, as it's so simple to have a small herb garden in lieu of buying the expensive and often-wilted supermarket herbs. In San Francisco I have a very small garden behind my house near Ocean Beach. These houses are built on the old sand dunes, and while the cold and fog are restrictive, the drainage is well suited for citrus roots. I rarely need to buy lemons or limes as my trees provide enough. In short, you can eliminate the need to purchase many of those higher-priced fruits and vegetables, particularly those that are used to add flavor to food. My land in Germany has dozens of apple and plum trees, along with peach, pear, cherry, redcurrant, blackcurrant, walnuts, and mulberry (both black and white). I process great vats of chutney and preserves in the summer, easily enough to share with my friends for the year.

However, it isn't always possible to have grapefruit trees or a patch of land large enough for potatoes and carrots, but a window box somewhere near the kitchen can make a few cilantro leaves readily available. Without going into the garden I have sage, oregano, chocolate, orange, and Moroccan mints, lovage, French sorrel, epazote, parsley, and thyme all in window boxes. This is virtually free food.

At the risk of being cutesy, various leaves and nutshells can replace landfill bound disposable items for a garden party. In Jaipur I noticed a street vendor using a hinged press device to form plates from a pile of leaves stacked next to his massive iron skillet. The plates were then used for a variety of fried snacks and chutney. After the samosas or pakoras were eaten, the plates were discarded, becoming food for any number of animals. It occurred to me that it is such a waste of resources to buy paper plates and straws for a party when such simple solutions are available.

Straws for fruit drinks

Angelica has a very pleasant taste, but raw it is a little bitter. This is quickly remedied by soaking the stems in sugar water. The perennial plant grows easily in a container and the leaves can be used for tea (page 209).

- 2 tablespoons sugar
- 1 cup water

- Long angelica stalks without joints

Dissolve the sugar in cold water. Wash and then soak the stalks in the sugar water for a couple of hours or overnight. These become perfect straws for fruit punch and can even be eaten afterward.

Plates

The classic southern Indian plate is the banana leaf. It will discolor with hot food and it is not suitable for liquid or runny food, but it's perfect in a party setting for samosas and chutney. Simply rinse off nicely shaped leaves and use whole. The spine offers some support down the center.

Fig leaves work much the same way, but of course they are considerably smaller. Use 3 or 4 stacked to insulate anything hot from your hand.

Recycled

Artichoke Stalk "Drumsticks"

Type: Indian
Speed: About 45 minutes
Notes: Drumsticks are a green tree pod used in vegetable and sambar recipes in India but are not widely available in the U.S. When the globe artichokes are in season the more succulent stalks can be selected to make mock drumsticks. The stalks resemble drumsticks visually, but unlike the real thing these can be completely eaten. To do so it is imperative that only the higher, softer stems are used to avoid a hard, fibrous outer layer.

- ½ a lemon, juiced
- 1 teaspoon salt
- 2 cups water
- ½ pound trimmed artichoke stalks
- 1 tablespoon oil
- 1 teaspoon cumin seeds
- 1 tablespoon coconut oil
- 1 large onion, thinly sliced into half rings

- 1 fresh green chile, finely chopped
- 1 teaspoon ground coriander
- 1 teaspoon brown sugar
- 1 teaspoon turmeric
- 1 teaspoon salt
- 1 teaspoon mango powder
- ½ teaspoon cayenne pepper
- 1 teaspoon garam masala

Prepare a saucepan with the lemon juice, salt, and water. Trim the outer skin from the artichoke stalks, taking care to remove the entire hard, fibrous layer. Then chop the stalks into 2-inch sticks and immediately drop them into the salt-lemon water. Remove the stalks to weigh them. Meanwhile, bring the saucepan to a boil. Return the stalks and boil them for 2 minutes. Turn off the heat and set the pot aside.

Heat the oil in an iron skillet. Once hot, add the cumin seeds. As soon as they sizzle add the coconut oil. Once it has melted, add the onion, reduce the heat to medium-low and stir. Drain the stalks and pat them dry with a paper towel and then add them to the skillet along with the fresh chile. Stir-fry for about 15 minutes, making sure the onion doesn't burn.

Add the coriander, sugar, turmeric, salt, mango powder, and cayenne. Stir for another 2 minutes before folding in the garam masala.

This is an excellent accompaniment for dal with some Indian bread.

Recycled

Banana Peel Relish

Type: South Indian
Speed: ½ hour
Notes: This is an interesting accompaniment to a southern Indian meal. The banana peel doesn't add too much bulk but adds an unusual secondary flavor.

- 1½ tablespoons oil
- ½ teaspoon cumin seeds
- ½ teaspoon black mustard seeds
- ¼ teaspoon asafetida
- 1 dry red chile pepper

- ½ teaspoon turmeric powder
- 2 tablespoons desiccated coconut
- 1 large tomato, finely chopped
- ¼ teaspoon salt
- 3 banana peels

Heat the oil in a skillet, then add the cumin and black mustard seeds. Once the seeds start to pop, add the asafetida and pepper and stir for a few seconds. Reduce the heat to low and add the turmeric and coconut. As soon as the coconut darkens, usually after only a few seconds, add the chopped tomato and salt. Cook until the tomato pieces collapse. Meanwhile, run a sharp knife between the soft white portion of the banana skin and the hard outer portion. Discard the outer skin and dice the white portion into small squares. Add the banana peel squares to the skillet and sauté until the mixture is fully cooked, about 10 minutes. Serve as a fresh relish, warm or cold, with southern Indian food.

> **Tip:** It is important, though using recycled peel, to use it as fresh as possible. After only a short time, once exposed to the air, the inside will turn dark. So perhaps you can cut the bananas into rounds and coat them with Orange Flower Syrup (page 23) for a kids' dessert and free the skins right when needed.

Recycled

Besan Scramble

Type: Indian
Speed: Very fast
Notes: Here's a way to use up either leftover Pakora batter (page 232) or leftover peas, onions, or mushrooms. Think of this like scrambled eggs for vegans. It is exceptionally easy to make and, as is common in the UK, you can use it as a toast topper or part of a more traditional breakfast.

- Leftover Pakora batter or ½ cup besan (chickpea flour)
- ½ teaspoon asafetida
- ½ teaspoon salt

One or more leftover portions of:

- Onions
- Peas
- Peppers
- Ginger
- Mushrooms
- Tomatoes
- Chives

Oil for frying

If you have leftover Pakora batter, simply water it down a little until it is the consistency of pancake batter.

Alternatively, mix the besan with the asafetida, salt, and enough water to make a smooth pancake batter.

Chop your leftovers finely (with the onions, hot peppers, ginger, and mushrooms) or a little coarser (tomatoes, chives, mild peppers). Peas can be left whole. Mix the leftovers into the batter.

In a nonstick frying pan, heat a little oil. Pour in the batter and scramble over high heat using a wooden spoon.

Black Vegetable Medley

Type: Arabian
Preparation: You will need ¼ cup of Black Olive Sauce (page 138) per 2 pounds of vegetables
Speed: Fast
Notes: A delicious way to use up the odd vegetables in the refrigerator is to use Black Olive Sauce. The great thing about this dish is it will always vary depending on which leftover vegetables are available. A nice touch is to finish the dish off in a tagine in the oven and serve straight to the table on a heat-resistant mat or pot stand. I have left the amounts of the vegetables to your discretion. You can be guided by how many people are being served, how much leftover vegetables you have, and how strongly flavored you like the dish.

This is also a good dish for the tagine (page 8). Pour about ½ cup of olive oil into the tray, then add all the raw vegetables with the black olive sauce. Add any cooked vegetables toward the end of cooking, then serve.

Choose from the following leftover vegetables:

- Brussels sprouts
- Cauliflower
- Parsnips
- Rutabagas
- Carrots

- Peas
- Green beans
- Fresh soybeans
- Chickpeas
- Grilled corn left on the cob

- ¼ cup Black Olive Sauce (page 138) per 2 pounds of cooked vegetables

- A little olive oil

If the vegetables are raw, bring a large saucepan of salt water to a boil and add the root vegetables and brussels sprouts. After 5 or so minutes, add the more delicate vegetables like cauliflower and green beans. When the vegetables are cooked through but still firm, drain and set aside. At this point you can add any leftover cooked vegetables.

Heat the black olive sauce in a large skillet. If it is raw, it takes 2 or 3 minutes of stirring. Fold in the vegetables, making sure the sauce is evenly distributed over them. Turn the vegetables until the flavors are absorbed. If you have leftover grilled corn, cut the cobs into 1½-inch segments and stir into the mix.

You shouldn't need any additional salt as the olive sauce is very salty. You can place into a serving bowl and add a drizzle of olive oil, or finish for a while in a tagine in the oven, ending again with a drizzle of olive oil. Serve hot with crusty bread or over couscous (page 127).

Recycled

Grilled Vegetables in Oil

Type: Mediterranean
Notes: Before I had any sort of kitchen at my German house, I rustled up meals on a camping stove and later a sandwich maker. I came up with a really easy way to make antipasti using a sandwich maker.

- Leftover red bell pepper
- Leftover fresh mushrooms
- Olive oil

- Salt
- Pepper

Set the sandwich maker on hot. Cut the red pepper and the mushrooms into strips. Arrange them on the sandwich maker and close the top. Char the peppers and mushrooms until they have lost most of their moisture but are not crisped. Remove them to a bowl and add a liberal amount of olive oil. Stir in salt and pepper to taste.

Option: You can add a little za'atar or Harissa (page 155) to the oil to spice it up.

Variation: I have used this method to make nettle antipasto. Cure the nettles in boiling water. Strain and remove the stalks. Wring out as much water as you can with your hands, then roll portions of the nettles into cigarette-sized logs. Char the logs in the sandwich maker until they are dried but not burnt. Reconstitute the nettles with olive oil and add salt and pepper to taste.

Recycled

Leftover Pasta

Type: North African
Preparation: You will need Black Olive Sauce (page 138)
Speed: Very fast
Notes: If you keep black olive sauce on hand in the refrigerator, you can rescue leftover pasta made for a party. Sometimes you might need to ease the pasta apart in water before you start the process, but in a matter of minutes you can produce an unusual pasta dish. Of course you can make this from scratch, but then don't forget to salt the water when boiling the pasta.

- Olive oil
- 1 small onion, chopped
- 1 tablespoon pine nuts
- 1 small green pepper, seeded and chopped

- Black Olive Sauce (page 138)
- 6 cups leftover pasta (or 12 ounces dry pasta)
- A few more pine nuts

Sauté the onions in the olive oil until golden brown. Add the pine nuts and green pepper, then stir on low heat for another few minutes. Stir in the black olive sauce (already fried for a few minutes) and continue to cook for a minute before adding the pasta, making sure it is coated with sauce. Transfer to bowls and garnish with a few pine nuts.

Recycled

Leftover Vegetable Korma

Type: Indian
Preparation: You will need North Indian Base Sauce (page 22) and White Nut Sauce (page 25)
Speed: Fast
Notes: Clear out those leftover vegetables and make a rich curry. You will need 2 pounds of vegetables. I like golden beets, green beans, carrots, potatoes, lotus root, peas, cauliflower, shallots, or any combination of vegetables you may have in the refrigerator.

- 2 pounds firm, cooked vegetables
- ¼ cup oil
- 2 tablespoons coconut oil
- 4 star anise
- 4 whole cloves
- 4 cardamom pods
- 4 bay leaves
- 1 teaspoon cumin
- 1 large onion, chopped
- 4 cloves garlic, chopped
- 2 tablespoons chopped fresh ginger
- 2 green chiles, chopped
- 1 tablespoon ground coriander
- 1 teaspoon turmeric
- 2 cups North Indian Base Sauce (page 22)
- 1 teaspoon garam masala
- 1 cup White Nut Sauce (page 25)
- 2 tablespoons fresh cilantro, chopped

Cut the root vegetables into cubes. Make sure to cook them first so they are cooked through but firm. You need to have a large saucepan with salted water. Bring to a boil, add the lotus root, and then the carrots, shallots, and beets. After about 5 minutes add things like potatoes, beans, and cauliflower.

   Heat the oils in a large saucepan. Add the anise, cloves, cardamom, and bay leaves. Let them sizzle for a couple of seconds, then add the cumin. After just a few seconds add the onion, garlic, ginger, and chiles. Fry until the onion is golden brown. Add the coriander and turmeric, then fold in the vegetables until they are coated with spices. Add the North Indian Base Sauce and fold it in, being careful not to break up the vegetables. Fold in the garam masala. Reduce the heat to low, mix in the nut sauce, and cook until it is warmed through. Place into a serving bowl and garnish with fresh cilantro.

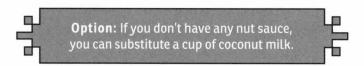

Option: If you don't have any nut sauce, you can substitute a cup of coconut milk.

Recycled

Lemon Peel and Onion Relish

Type: Indian
Speed: Fast
Notes: This fresh relish will be scorching hot if you use a strong cayenne pepper such as African bird's eye. It is a good accompaniment to rice and perhaps dal.

- 1 medium lemon, peeled
- 1 small onion, coarsely chopped
- ½ teaspoon salt
- 1 tablespoon cayenne pepper
- 1 tablespoon paprika
- 2 tablespoons oil
- Pinch of Indian black salt (optional)

Chop the lemon peel coarsely and mix it in a bowl with the chopped onion. Sprinkle on the salt and let stand for 10 minutes. Combine the cayenne and paprika in a small bowl.

Heat the oil in a small saucepan until almost smoking. Tip the pepper powder into the oil and stir quickly with a wooden spatula. Scrape the contents onto the lemon peel-onion mixture in the bowl. Mix in the spiced oil until it is thoroughly combined. Sprinkle on the black salt and mix it in. Serve in a small relish bowl.

Recycled

Miner's Lettuce Salad

Type: Arabian
Preparation: You must gather a bag of wild miner's lettuce
Speed: Quick
Notes: This green salad grows abundantly here in California and is said to have been used by the San Francisco gold rush miners to combat scurvy. It can be found along the entire West Coast, but for those who can't find it, lamb's lettuce (mâche) makes a good substitute.

- 4 ounces miner's lettuce
- 1 tablespoon pine nuts
- ¼ Preserved Lemon (page 165)
- 1 tablespoon olive oil
- 1 tablespoon capers
- Pinch of salt
- Pinch of ground black pepper
- 1 small bunch of chives, chopped
- 1 tablespoon sumac powder

Wash and trim the greens. I like to remove the flower and cut the stalk to ½ inch, as it can be slightly stringy. Place the greens in a colander to drain. Dry roast the pine nuts until they lightly char, then set them aside to cool on a plate. Slice the lemon and place it in a small bowl with the oil. Crush the lemon into the oil with a fork, then add the capers, salt, and pepper. Place the greens in a large bowl, mix in the chives, and fold in the oil dressing. Toss until the greens are coated, then place in a decorative serving bowl and sprinkle on the sumac, or add the sumac and toss the salad before dividing onto individual plates.

This lively green salad goes well with hummus and pita for a light lunch.

Nasturtium Seed Pickle

Type: Indian/Arabian
Preparation: 3 days soaking. Ready to use after 3 months.
Speed: Fast
Notes: The seeds of the nasturtium plant are very strong and peppery. They look like ridged peas and usually appear in threes on the vine-like runners. They are easy to harvest where great walls of the plant grow up into bushes and small trees. Harvest only the fresh, full-sized green seeds. After pickling, you can use them like capers.

- 1 pound nasturtium seeds
- 3 cups water (times 3)
- ¼ cup salt (times 3)
- 1 bulb of garlic with small cloves
- 3 cups white wine vinegar
- 1 tablespoon whole cloves
- 2 tablespoons coarsely chopped ginger
- 3 bay leaves
- 1 tablespoon ground mace
- 12 small chile peppers, slit lengthwise

Wash the seeds in several changes of water and remove any stalks and debris. Place the seeds in a large bowl and fill with salt water. Rinse the seeds each day and refill with salt water for 3 days.

On the fourth day, drain, rinse, and dry the seeds. Break the garlic into cloves, then skin and trim the end. In a large saucepan, bring the vinegar to a boil and add the garlic as well as the rest of the ingredients except the nasturtium seeds to the pan and then simmer for 10 minutes. Decide on the size and number of jars and sterilize them with boiling water. Dry the jars completely. With a slotted spoon, scoop the boiled spice into the bowl of seeds and distribute them evenly. Then transfer the mixture into the jars. Make sure each jar has some garlic, ginger, cloves, and peppers. Reheat the vinegar and fill the jars, covering the seeds. Seal the jars and store for 3 months before using.

Recycled

Nettle Saag

Type: North Indian
Preparation: Collect a large bag of fresh stinging nettles, about 1½ pounds
Speed: About 45 minutes
Notes: Stinging nettles are an often-overlooked free green. At the height of the growing season they can be chest high and restrict areas of the garden. When you clear a patch, try this North Indian dish in place of spinach. You will need to handle them with gloves until you blanch them for a minute in boiling water.

- 1½ pounds stinging nettles
- 1 tablespoon oil
- 1 teaspoon cumin seeds
- 2 tablespoons coconut oil
- 1 clove of garlic, finely chopped
- 1 green chile, finely chopped

- 2 medium potatoes, peeled and cut into dice-sized cubes
- ¼ teaspoon ginger powder
- 1 teaspoon salt
- 1 cup water
- ½ teaspoon garam masala

Collect fresh, bright green nettles with large leaves using a plastic bag and wearing gloves. You can use a garden hose to spray the nettles, removing any bugs before bringing them to the kitchen. Keeping the gloves on, remove the large stalks.

Bring a large saucepan of water to a boil, then dunk all of the nettles in and boil for about a minute. Remove the greens to a colander to drain.

Heat the oil in a skillet and add the cumin seeds. As soon as they start to sizzle, add the coconut oil. After the coconut oil melts add the garlic and ginger. Sizzle for a few seconds and add the potato cubes. Stir-fry the potato on low heat until the cubes take on a golden color, about 2 or 3 minutes. Be careful not to burn the garlic. Sprinkle on the ginger and salt.

Squeeze out any excess water from the greens with your hands. They are now safe to touch, as the acid is destroyed in the hot water. Loosen the mass of greens as you drop them into the skillet. Fold the mixture to make sure everything is coated with oil and spices. Add the water and bring to a boil. Reduce the heat to low and cover. Simmer for 5 minutes.

Remove the lid and continue to heat to dry out the saag a little. Fold the mixture carefully to avoid burning the bottom. Mix in the garam masala and serve.

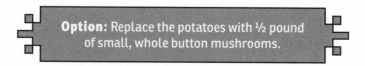

Option: Replace the potatoes with ½ pound of small, whole button mushrooms.

Nettle Soup

Type: Indian
Preparation: Collect a large bag of fresh stinging nettles, about 1½ pounds. You will also need vegetable stock (page 17).
Speed: About 45 minutes

- 1½ pounds stinging nettles
- 2 tablespoons oil
- 1 large onion, chopped
- 2 clove of garlic, chopped
- ¼ teaspoon black pepper
- ¼ teaspoon ground nutmeg
- ¼ teaspoon ground cloves
- 3 cups vegetable stock
- 1 cup coconut milk
- ¼ cup coconut cream
- 1 tablespoon salt
- ½ a lemon, juiced
- 1 tablespoon oil
- 1 teaspoon black mustard seeds
- ½ teaspoon cumin seeds
- 2 fresh red chiles, destalked and slit lengthwise
- 10 fresh curry leaves

Collect fresh, bright green nettles with large leaves using a plastic bag and wearing gloves. Make sure to spray off any bugs and cuckoo spit (a white foam that protects bugs), which is often on nettles. Remove the larger stalks while still wearing gloves. Bring a large saucepan of water to a boil , dunk in the greens, and boil for a minute. Put the nettles into a colander to drain.

Heat the oil in a large saucepan and add the onion and garlic. Fry while stirring for about 5 minutes. Now add the pepper, nutmeg, and cloves. Stir for another minute and turn off the heat. Add a cup of the stock and pour the contents into the food processor. Blend to a smooth sauce and return to the saucepan along with the rest of the stock. Bring it to a boil and add the coconut milk, coconut cream, salt, and lemon juice. Simmer for a minute and turn off the heat. Heat the oil in a skillet and when it's hot add the mustard seeds. Once they start popping add the cumin, chiles, and curry leaves. As soon as the cumin sizzles and the peppers turn a few shades darker, scrape the contents into the soup, mix it in, and serve in small bowls.

Tip: You can substitute spinach for the nettles.

Recycled

Pakoras

Type: Indian
Speed: Less than an hour
Notes: I've included pakoras in the Recycled section because they are the best way I know to use up odds and ends from the refrigerator. Cauliflower, potatoes, peppers, carrots, asparagus, even green bananas can be turned into appetizers.

- 1 cup besan (chickpea flour)
- ¼ teaspoon cayenne pepper
- ¼ teaspoon turmeric
- 1 teaspoon ground coriander
- ½ teaspoon garam masala
- ½ teaspoon salt
- ½ cup cold water
- Oil for deep frying

Sieve the besan into a bowl and mix in the other dry spices. Now add the water and beat until it is smooth. It should be quite thick. Let the mixture stand for half an hour.

Dip thinly sliced vegetables in the batter and deep fry them until they are cooked through and the batter is a golden brown. Make sure the vegetable pieces are not too thick or the batter will burn before the inside of the vegetable is cooked.

Lay the pakoras out on a paper towel before serving on a dish with Tamarind Dipping Sauce (page 168) and Mint Chutney (page 161).

Pepper Broth

Type: South Indian
Speed: About an hour
Notes: There are thousands of different recipes for rasam and Indian pepper water. The thin broth is usually quite fiery, often utilizing whole hot peppers in the tempering stage. For those used to this type of food, it is not surprising. Others will often say, "@#$%, I just bit into something really hot." In this recipe I've created an authentic rasam using the soaking water from making Harissa (page 155). Here the complex flavors and heat coexist without the capsicum sea mines. You can replace the pepper water with plain water and ½ teaspoon of cayenne pepper, but either way keep the simmer low to not evaporate too much water. The soup should be thin, so add a little more water before tempering if needed. This is enough for 4 to 6 small starter bowls.

- ¼ cup toor dal, rinsed
- 2 cups water
- Pepper water from Harissa (page 155) (about 4 cups)
- 1 large tomato, peeled and diced
- ½ teaspoon salt
- ½ teaspoon tamarind concentrate
- ¼ teaspoon turmeric
- 1½ teaspoon coriander seeds
- ½ teaspoon black peppercorns
- 2 dried curry leaves
- 1 cup more water
- 1 tablespoon oil
- 1 teaspoon black mustard seeds
- ½ teaspoon cumin seeds
- ½ teaspoon asafetida
- 4 fresh curry leaves
- 1 tablespoon fresh cilantro leaves, chopped, for garnish

Bring the water to a boil with the dal, cover, and reduce the heat to a low simmer for 30 minutes. Add the pepper water, tomato, salt, tamarind, and turmeric, keeping it simmering. Dry roast the coriander and black pepper, then grind the seeds along with the curry leaves in a spice grinder.

Add the spice mixture to the pan with another cup of water and simmer on low for 20 minutes.

When the dal is finished, mash it with a fork or potato masher and let it continue to simmer.

Heat the oil in a small frying pan until it's very hot. Add the mustard and cumin seeds. As soon as they start sputtering, add the asafetida and curry leaves. Stir and add the contents to the soup. Bring it to a boil, then pour it into bowls and garnish with cilantro leaves.

Roasted Squash/ Pumpkin Seeds

Type: Indian/Arabian
Speed: Fast
Notes: Instead of just throwing out squash seeds, why not roast them? In Arab countries this type of roasted seed is very popular and you will often see piles of shells on the sidewalk. You can eat the shell, but most people split them open by applying pressure with their front teeth on the pointed edges. In this way you will still get the taste of the spices as you open them. I have given Indian and Arabian flavoring options.

- About 5 ounces squash or pumpkin seeds
- ½ teaspoon salt
- ¼ teaspoon paprika
- ¼ teaspoon garam masala for Indian or ¼ teaspoon cayenne pepper for Arabian

Preheat the oven to 260°F.

Take the center fibers and seeds from your barbecued squash or pumpkin and drop them into a large bowl of water (see tip below). Remove any flesh clinging to the seeds and transfer them to a colander. Mix the other ingredients together in a small bowl. Once the seeds have drained but are still moist, transfer them to a bowl and toss them in the spice mixture.

Lay the seasoned seeds on a baking tray and place them in the oven. They will need to roast for about 45 minutes. Transfer to a bowl to cool.

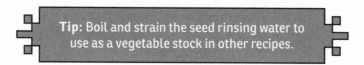

Tip: Boil and strain the seed rinsing water to use as a vegetable stock in other recipes.

Vegetable Curry Dal

Type: South Indian
Speed: Less than an hour
Notes: Here's another way to gather odds and sods from the vegetable drawer and turn them into a filling main dish.

- 1½ pounds mixed vegetables cut into 1-inch cubes (for example potato, cauliflower, carrot, green beans, etc.)
- 1 cup red lentils (masoor dal)
- ½ cup moong dal
- 3 tablespoons unsweetened desiccated coconut
- ¼ cup vegetable oil
- 1 teaspoon black mustard seeds
- 1 teaspoon cumin seeds
- ½ teaspoon asafetida
- 1-inch stick cassia or cinnamon
- 3 dry red chile peppers
- 12 curry leaves
- 3 cloves garlic, minced
- 3 cups water
- 1 teaspoon turmeric
- 3 tablespoons Sambar Powder (page 20)
- 2 cups tomatoes, thickly cut
- 1 tablespoon salt
- 1 teaspoon tamarind paste, dissolved in ¼ cup warm water
- ¼ cup oil
- 1 teaspoon fenugreek seed
- 3 cloves garlic, sliced
- 2 tablespoons fresh cilantro leaves, chopped

Rinse both dals together in several changes of water until the water is no longer cloudy. Drain and set aside. Prepare the vegetables and place in a bowl of water until needed (then drain). Dry roast the coconut until it is a cinnamon color. Grind in a mortar and pestle and set aside.

Heat the oil in a large saucepan, then add the mustard and cumin seeds. When the mustard starts to pop reduce the heat to medium-low and sprinkle on the asafetida immediately followed by the cassia (or cinnamon), red peppers, curry leaves, garlic, and roasted coconut powder. Stir for a minute while the garlic darkens. Add the water, drained dal, turmeric, and sambar powder. Cover and bring to a boil, then reduce the heat to low and simmer until the dal breaks down, about 10 minutes. Add the bowl of vegetables, tomatoes, salt, and tamarind water. Bring back to a boil, then reduce the heat and continue to cook on low heat until the vegetables are cooked (the time will vary depending on which vegetables you are using).

Heat the remaining oil in a small frying pan and add fenugreek and garlic, then stir and add the cilantro. After they sizzle for a few seconds and the garlic is golden, pour the contents over the dal, fold in, and serve.

Vegetables with Apricots

Type: Moroccan
Preparation: You will need Barbecue Sauce (page 138)
Speed: Less than an hour
Notes: This casserole is a good way to use up the odd vegetables in the refrigerator using Barbecue Sauce. It is perfect served over couscous (page 127). This kind of dish is also a perfect candidate for tagine cooking (page 8).

- 1½ pounds leftover vegetables (for example brussels sprouts, cauliflower, carrots, celery root, green beans, grilled corn left on the cob, etc.)
- ½ cup dried (unsulphered) apricots
- 1 tablespoon salt
- 2 tablespoons oil
- 1 small onion, chopped
- 2 cloves garlic, chopped
- ¼ cup Barbecue Sauce (page 138)

Bring a large saucepan of salt water to a boil and add the brussels sprouts and carrots. After about 5 minutes, add the cauliflower, green beans, and apricots. When the vegetables are cooked through but still firm, drain and set them aside.

Heat oil in large skillet, then add the onion and garlic. Fry on a low heat until golden brown. Stir in the barbecue sauce. When the sauce is evenly distributed and is sizzling, stir in the drained vegetables. Mix the vegetables until fully coated. If you have leftover grilled corn, cut the cobs into 1½-inch segments and stir into the mix. Make sure the corn is heated through. Check the saltiness before serving.

Watermelon Rind Bharta

Type: Indian
Speed: Less than an hour
Notes: You will need about ⅓ of the rind from a large watermelon for this creamy bharta.

- 2 cups grated watermelon rind
- ¼ cup vegetable oil
- ½ teaspoon cumin seeds
- ½ teaspoon black mustard seed
- 1 large onion, chopped
- 2 cloves garlic, finely chopped
- 1 tablespoon finely chopped fresh ginger
- 1 green chile pepper, minced
- 1 teaspoon garam masala
- 1 teaspoon salt
- ½ teaspoon turmeric
- ½ teaspoon cayenne pepper
- ½ cup coconut milk
- Fresh cilantro leaves for garnish

Cut the watermelon rind into strips and remove the green skin with a sharp knife. Make sure all of the red watermelon is removed from the other side. Grate the rind into a bowl, then squeeze out most of the juice with your hands. Heat the oil in a large skillet, then add cumin and mustard seed. As soon as they start popping add the onion, garlic, ginger, and chile. Fry on medium-low heat until the onion is golden brown, about 10 minutes. Add the rind and fry for another 10 minutes while stirring. The rind should start to darken a little. Mix in the garam masala, salt, turmeric, and cayenne pepper. Continue to fry for another 2 minutes while stirring. Mix in the coconut milk and simmer for another 10 minutes. The bharta should start to dry out a little. Serve hot, garnished with some chopped cilantro leaves.

Recycled

About the Author

Born in Leicestershire, England, in 1955, Nicky Garratt is an internationally recognized guitar player. Best known as a founding member of the seminal punk band UK Subs, he subsequently moved to the USA, built the record label New Red Archives, and has been involved in many diverse music projects.

Over the past forty years he has been an outspoken advocate for science and animal rights, and is active on the lecture circuit on science advocacy topics. He now spends time between homes in San Francisco and Quedlinburg, Germany.

Für den hasen nicht den Jäger

Index by Cuisine

Index by Cuisine

Index

Index

Alternative Vegan
International Vegan Fare Straight from the Produce Aisle
Dino Sarma Weierman
$17.95 • 160 pages

ALTERNATIVE VEGAN

"I want you to look at the recipes presented here and be as excited as a kid with a new toy. I want your heart to race, your mouth to water, and your pots and pans to sing to you as they bring together the elements of a good dining experience . . ."
—From the Introduction

Tofu, seitan, tempeh, tofu, seitan, tempeh . . . it seems like so many vegans rely on these products as meat substitutes. Isn't it time to break out of the mold? Taking a fresh, bold, and alternative approach to vegan cooking without the substitutes, this cookbook showcases more than 100 fully vegan recipes, many of which have South Asian influences. With a jazz-style approach to cooking, it also discusses how to improvise cooking with simple ingredients and how to stock a kitchen to prepare simple and delicious vegan meals quickly. The recipes for mouth-watering dishes include one-pot meals—such as South-Indian Uppama and Chipotle Garlic Risotto along with Pakoras, Flautas, Bajji, Kashmiri Biriyani, Hummus Canapes, and No-Cheese Pizza. With new, improved recipes this updated edition also shows how to cook simply to let the flavor of fresh ingredients shine through.

Explore your inner chef and get cooking with Dino!

"This is vegan new school, which is really vegan old school, which draws on traditions that pre-date any of us. Cooking can be empowering, no doubt about it."
—Lauren Corman, host of Animal Voices on CIUT in Toronto.

Dino Sarma Weierman was born in New Delhi, India, and immigrated to the USA with his family in 1986. From childhood, cooking has been a passion for him. He draws his influences from his mother and the many hours of food shows on television that he watched. Dino also writes and podcasts about food at altveg.blogspot.com.

NEW AMERICAN VEGAN

New American Vegan
Vincent Guihan
$17.95 • 240 pages

All across North America, people are looking to make better choices, but also eat healthier, more environmentally friendly and, most of all, great-tasting food. *New American Vegan* breaks from a steady stream of cookbooks inspired by fusion and California cuisines that put catchy titles and esoteric ingredients first in their efforts to cater to a cosmopolitan taste. Instead, Vincent goes back to his Midwestern roots to play a humble but important role in the reinvention of American cuisine while bringing the table back to the center of American life.

Weaving together small town values, personal stories and over 100 great recipes, *New American Vegan* delivers authentically American food that simply has to be tasted to be believed. Recipes range from very basic to the modestly complicated, but always with an eye on creating something that is both beautiful and delicious while keeping it simple. Clear instructions provide step by steps, but also help new cooks find their feet in the kitchen, with a whole chapter devoted just to terms, tools and techniques. With an eye towards improvisation, the book provides a detailed basic recipe that's good as-is, but also provides additional notes that explain how to take each recipe further, to increase flavor, to add drama to the presentation or just how to add a little extra flourish for new cooks and seasoned kitchen veterans.

> "Guihan has a knack for infusing bold and fiery seasonings into fresh produce and vegan pantry staples—creating inventive, novel recipes that will inspire and excite the vegan home cook."
> —Dreena Burton, author of *Eat, Drink & Be Vegan*

Vincent has been a vegan for more than a decade, and was a lacto-ovo vegetarian for a decade prior to becoming vegan. He grew up in a in a very small Midwestern town (Warterman, IL), where his back yard was the neighbor's cornfield. His parents cooked only sporadically, even though the nearest fast-food restaurants were a 20-minute car ride away and this cookbook is his revenge. Raised on TV dinners, burgers, pizza and spaghetti, he spent much of his young adulthood nestled between the delicatessens, greasy spoons and taquerias of Chicago's southwest side, which helped to build his palate. Today, he lives in Ottawa, Canada, a city renowned (at least in Canada!) for its cosmopolitan snugness in spite of its size where he gorges himself on the cornucopia of foods from all over the globe, many of which he can't even pronounce. He blogs about vegan cooking and gourmet topics at www.applepickersunion.com. And although not a formally trained chef, he's a formally trained and highly skilled eater.

COOK, EAT, THRIVE

Cook, Eat, Thrive
Vegan Recipes from Everyday to Exotic
Joy Tienzo
$17.95 • 256 pages

"Whether we find ourselves living large or small, everyday or exotic, there are countless opportunities to come to the table."
—From the introduction

In *Cook, Eat, Thrive*, Joy Tienzo encourages you to savor the cooking process while crafting distinctive meals from fresh, flavorful ingredients. Enjoy comfortable favorites. Broaden your culinary horizons with internationally-inspired dishes. Share with friends and family, and create cuisine that allows people, animals, and the environment to fully thrive.

Cook, Eat, Thrive features dishes from both the everyday and the exotic.

- Buttermilk Biscuits with Southern Style Gravy
- Earl Grey Carrot Muffins
- Orange Cream Green Smoothie
- Palm Heart Ceviche
- Barbecue Ranch Salad
- Riz et Pois Rouges
- Raspberry Chèvre Salad with Champagne Vinaigrette
- Samosa Soup
- Ras el Hanout Roasted Beets

- Tarte aux Poireaux et Pommes de Terre
- Mofongo with Cilantro Lime Gremolata
- Italian Cornmeal Cake with Roasted Apricots and Coriander Crème Anglaise
- Lavender Rice Pudding Brulee with Blueberries
- Peanut Butter Shortbread with Concord Grape Sorbet

Inside, you'll also find:

- An extensive equipment and ingredients listing
- Basics like seitan, non-dairy milks, grains, frozen desserts, and salad dressing
- Menus for occasions, from Caribbean-inspired garden parties to vegan weddings
- Practical symbols to let you know if recipes are raw, low fat, soy-free, wheat-free, approachable for non-vegans, and quick fix

"*Cook, Eat, Thrive* gives vegans the option of choosing exotic and extraordinary recipes for special dinner preparations, or simpler, yet imaginative creations for day to day meal planning. Whether you're looking for everyday vegan fare, or exquisite vegan dining, Tienzo serves it up with culinary flair!"
—Dreena Burton, author of Eat, Drink & Be Vegan

Joy Tienzo loves food, and writing about food. Whether working as a pastry cook, hosting community brunches, or crafting wedding cakes, her purpose in life is to feed as many people as well as possible. When not in the kitchen, Joy can be found on a plane, a yoga mat, or volunteering for refugee and human rights causes. She lives in Denver with her husband and daughter, and can be found online at www.JoyTienzo.com.

About PM Press

PM Press was founded at the end of 2007 by a small collection of folks with decades of publishing, media, and organizing experience. PM Press co-conspirators have published and distributed hundreds of books, pamphlets, CDs, and DVDs. Members of PM have founded enduring book fairs, spearheaded victorious tenant organizing campaigns, and worked closely with bookstores, academic conferences, and even rock bands to deliver political and challenging ideas to all walks of life. We're old enough to know what we're doing and young enough to know what's at stake.

We seek to create radical and stimulating fiction and non-fiction books, pamphlets, T-shirts, visual and audio materials to entertain, educate and inspire you. We aim to distribute these through every available channel with every available technology—whether that means you are seeing anarchist classics at our bookfair stalls; reading our latest vegan cookbook at the café; downloading geeky fiction e-books; or digging new music and timely videos from our website.

PM Press is always on the lookout for talented and skilled volunteers, artists, activists and writers to work with. If you have a great idea for a project or can contribute in some way, please get in touch.

PM Press
PO Box 23912
Oakland CA 94623
510-658-3906
www.pmpress.org

Friends of PM

These are indisputably momentous times—the financial system is melting down globally and the Empire is stumbling. Now more than ever there is a vital need for radical ideas.

In the six years since its founding—and on a mere shoestring—PM Press has risen to the formidable challenge of publishing and distributing knowledge and entertainment for the struggles ahead. With over 250 releases to date, we have published an impressive and stimulating array of literature, art, music, politics, and culture. Using every available medium, we've succeeded in connecting those hungry for ideas and information to those putting them into practice.

Friends of PM allows you to directly help impact, amplify, and revitalize the discourse and actions of radical writers, filmmakers, and artists. It provides us with a stable foundation from which we can build upon our early successes and provides a much-needed subsidy for the materials that can't necessarily pay their own way. You can help make that happen—and receive every new title automatically delivered to your door once a month—by joining as a Friend of PM Press. And, we'll throw in a free T-shirt when you sign up.

Here are your options:

- $25 a month: Get all books and pamphlets plus 50% discount on all webstore purchases
- $40 a month: Get all PM Press releases (including CDs and DVDs) plus 50% discount on all webstore purchases
- $100 a month: Superstar—Everything plus PM merchandise, free downloads, and 50% discount on all webstore purchases

For those who can't afford $25 or more a month, we're introducing Sustainer Rates at $15, $10, and $5. Sustainers get a free PM Press T-shirt and a 50% discount on all purchases from our website.

Your Visa or Mastercard will be billed once a month, until you tell us to stop. Or until our efforts succeed in bringing the revolution around. Or the financial meltdown of Capital makes plastic redundant. Whichever comes first.